Palgrave Studies in Masculinity, Sport and Exercise

Series Editors
Rory Magrath, Southampton Solent University, Southampton,
Hampshire, UK
Jamie Cleland, University of South Australia, Adelaide, Australia
Eric Anderson, University of Winchester, Winchester, UK

Recent years have seen the emergence of a considerable body of research investigating the complex nature of masculinity, and how it impacts on a wide-range of sporting (and exercise) cultures. Palgrave Studies in Masculinity, Sport and Exercise is the first series solely dedicated to providing innovative and high-quality scholarship within this area of study. The series welcomes proposals for research monographs, Palgrave Pivots and edited collections examining critical, empirical and theoretical issues related to the study of masculinity, sport and exercise. The series has an international focus—both in terms of its authorship and readership— and welcomes relevant scholarship by established and emerging scholars in the field from any country.

More information about this series at
https://link.springer.com/bookseries/16505

Joaquín Piedra · Eric Anderson
Editors

Lesbian, Gay, and Transgender Athletes in Latin America

palgrave
macmillan

Editors
Joaquín Piedra
Universidad de Sevilla
Sevilla, Spain

Eric Anderson
University of Winchester
Winchester, UK

ISSN 2662-740X   ISSN 2662-7418   (electronic)
Palgrave Studies in Masculinity, Sport and Exercise
ISBN 978-3-030-87374-5   ISBN 978-3-030-87375-2   (eBook)
https://doi.org/10.1007/978-3-030-87375-2

CONTENTS

Notes on Contributors

Eric Anderson is Professor of Sport, Masculinities and Sexualities at the University of Winchester, UK. He is considered an expert on the experiences of gay men in sport and has published several Palgrave books: including, *21st Century Jocks, Discovering Sociology, The Palgrave Handbook on Sport and Masculinity.* He holds four degrees, has published 21 books, and over 70 peer-reviewed journal articles. His research is regularly featured in international television, print and digital media.

Oswaldo Ceballos-Gurrola holds Ph.D. in physical activity and sports sciences from the University of Zaragoza, Spain. He is full-time professor-researcher and ex-director of the School of Sports Organization, UANL (Mexico). He is Member of the National System of Researchers-level 2, President of the Latin American Association of Sports Science, Physical Education and Dance, Vice President of the Board of Directors of the Mexican Association of Higher Institutions of Physical Culture. He is also author of different books, articles, book chapters related to physical education and physical activity and health.

Alex Channon is a Senior Lecturer in Physical Education and Sport Studies at the University of Brighton, having previously taught at Loughborough University, the University of Greenwich and Syracuse University. He teaches on undergraduate courses, covering topics including sociological aspects of PE and sport, and qualitative research methods, and UK PE and sport policy. Alex's research interests are focused on martial arts, particularly exploring issues related to gender and embodiment. More recently, he has also explored the representation of women and sexual minority men in sports media.

José Devís-Devís is Professor in "Physical Education and Sports" and coordinates the "Physical Activity, Education and Society" research group at the Universitat de València (Spain). He obtained the Baccalaurate in the INEF-Universidad Politécnica de Madrid and the Ph.D. in the Universitat de València. He is currently developing quantitative and qualitative research in Physical Education and Physical Education Teacher Education, as well as in leisure time physical activity in different vulnerable groups such as people with disabilities and trans persons. He is member of the first Spanish research network on sport and people LGBTI+.

Alexandre Fernández-Vaz holds Ph.D. in Human and Social Sciences. Alexandre is Professor of the Postgraduate Program in Education and of the Interdisciplinary Postgraduate Program in Human Sciences at the Federal University of Santa Catarina (UFSC), in Florianópolis, Brazil and Researcher of the National Council for Scientific and Technological Development (CNPq). Núcleo de Estudos e Pesquisas Educação e Sociedade Contemporânea—UFSC/UFRJ/CNPq. He is also Member of the Working Group CLACSO Sport, Culture and Society.

Rafael García-Pérez is a Senior Lecturer in the Faculty of Educational Sciences at Universidad de Sevilla (Spain). As an expert in research methods and gender perspective he has published dozens of papers and chapters about education, sociology and sport. Rafael is member of the research group Development and Innovation of Educational Models at Universidad de Sevilla.

Javier Gil-Quintana is Lecturer at the Faculty of Physical Activity and Sports Sciences of the University of Valencia and at the International University of La Rioja (UNIR). He has a Ph.D. in Physical Activity and Sports Sciences at the University of the Basque Country (UPV-EHU) and is a member of the research group "Physical Activity, Education and Society" and in "Soca-Rel", a critical physical education seminar. He is member of the first Spanish research network on sport and people LGBTI+ and is President of the LGBTI Sport Club Samarucs Valencia.

George Jennings is a British qualitative sociologist interested in alternative physical culture: physical culture understood as both as the study of different ways to embody and live human movement, and methods to study them. He has a particular interest in traditionalist body cultures and martial arts/combat sports and is currently exploring the recently created fighting systems of Mexico alongside a broader study of the dynamic relationships between martial arts, health and society. George collaborates widely and has worked at universities in England, Scotland and Mexico. Currently, he is Lecturer in Sport Sociology and Physical Culture at Cardiff Metropolitan University.

Jorge Knijnik is a Brazilian-Australian academic currently working at Western Sydney University (NSW, Australia), where he is an Associate Professor in the School of Education and a researcher in the Institute for Culture and Society. He holds a Ph.D. in Social Psychology by Universidade de São Paulo (SP-Brazil). Dr. Knijnik's most recent books are: *The World Cup Chronicles: 31 Days that Rocked Brazil* (Fair Play Publishing); *Embodied Masculinities in Global Sport* (with Daryl Adair, FIT); *Gender and Equestrian Sports: Riding Around the World* (with Miriam Adelman, Springer); *Gênero e Esporte: masculinidades e feminilidades* (Rio de Janeiro, Apicuri); *Meninas e meninos na Educação Física: gênero e corporeidade no século 21* (São Paulo, Fontoura).

Vinnicius Laurindo is a Ph.D. student in the postgraduate program in Physical Education at UFES/Brazil (University of Espírito Santo). He is currently a Physical Education teacher at Espírito Santo. He has experience in Education, with an emphasis on Physical Education mainly on the following topics: Physical Education in Basic Education; Gender representations and identities. He is member of Grupa/UFES (Group of Studies in Gender and Sport), interested in acting in the areas of socio-cultural phenomena applied to Physical Education and Sport; Gender, Sexualities and Queer Studies and Athletes' Sports Career Trajectory (especially Volleyball and Beach Volleyball).

Jeanette Magnolia López-Walle has Ph.D. in Physical Activity and Health from the University of Granada, and Postdoc in the Research Unit in Sports Psychology (UIPD) of the University of Valencia, Spain. He is full-time professor-researcher and Vice Principal of Planning of the School of Sports Organization, UANL. He is Member of the National System of Researchers (SNI) level 2; leader of the consolidated academic body "Sciences of Physical Culture and Sport" (UANL-CA-306); and leader of the International Network "Sciences of Physical Activity, Sport and Education".

Mariana Zuaneti Martins is professor of Sports Department at University of Espírito Santo (UFES/Brazil), where she coordinates GRUPA (Group of Studies in Gender and Sport). Dr. Martins holds a bachelor's degree in Social Science and Physical Education from University of Campinas (UNICAMP), a master's degree in Physical Education from Unicamp/Brazil and a Ph.D. in Physical Education from Unicamp/Brazil. Previously she held faculty positions at the Institute of Science and Technology of South of Minas Gerais/Brazil (2014–2016). She is an advisor at graduate level in Physical Education at University of Espírito Santo and member of Gender Work Group from Brazilian College of Sports Science. In recent years, Dr. Martins' line of research stems from gender relations on sports to sociology of sports in general.

Rosa Elena Medina-Rodríguez is Doctor of Economic and Business Sciences form the University of Zaragoza, Spain. He is full-time professor-researcher of the School of Sports Organization, UANL (Mexico) and President of the Latin American Association of Sports Management. He is author of different books, articles, book chapters related to sport management.

Joan Miró as a closeted gay person playing football and due to the lack of models in sports, he never felt completely comfortable until he joined a gay football club in Berlin where he was living in 1994. It was such a good experience that when he went back to Barcelona created the football section of Panteres Grogues, the only existing gay sports club in Spain, which had started only a few months before. In 2000 he became President of the club, where he stayed in office for 9 years. During his presidency, the club grew from 4 sports and around 50 members to become the organizer of the EuroGames 2008 in Barcelona, this event with more than 5.000 participants was awarded by the European Gay and Lesbian Football Association. He also had time to be President of the IGLFA (International Gay and Lesbian Football Association) from 2003 to 2005 and was one of the founders of ADI (Agrupación Deportiva Ibérica LGTB) in 2009, where he was the first President serving until 2015. His personal experience moved him to be one of the main advocates to fight against homophobia in sports in Spain during the time he served as President of Panteres Grogues, IGLFA and ADI, as well as Vice President of the Barcelona LGTB City Council.

Sofía Pereira-García is a Lecturer at the Universitat de València (Spain) in the Faculty of Social Sciences. She participates in a research team called "Physical Activity, Education and Society" and in "Soca-Rel", a critical physical education seminar. Her research interests are related to queer pedagogy, embodiment and physical education with vulnerable groups, such as trans people. She is currently developing qualitative research regarding these topics. She is also a member of the first research network focused on sport and LGBTI+ people in Spain.

Magalí Pérez-Riedel is an Argentinian Ph.D. student at National University of La Plata and researcher in genders, sexualities, discrimination and online communication. She is the author of the book *Gender and sexual diversity in the blog Boquitas Pintadas* [original title: *Género y diversidad sexual en el blog Boquitas Pintadas*].

Joaquín Piedra is a specialist in the analysis of sport from the gender perspective. He is author in 2016 of the book *Gender and Sport: Handbook for Beginners*. He is also coordinator of the books *Gender, Masculinity and Diversity: Physical Education, Sport and Masculine Identities* in 2013 and *Physical Co-education: Contributions for a New Gender Culture* in 2014. He has also participated in research projects with public funding on Homophobia in Physical Education and Sport in Spain, the history of female athletes during Franco's dictatorship, as well as projects on co-education in the classroom. He has been a visiting researcher at University of Barry (USA), University of Greenwich (UK), University of Porto (Portugal) and Complutense University of Madrid (Spain). He is member of the first Spanish research network on sport and people LGBTI+.

Luis Tomás Ródenas-Cuenca holds Ph.D. in Physical Activity and Sport Sciences from the University of Valencia (Spain). He is full-time Professor Holder "A" at the Autonomous University of Nuevo León (UANL) and Member of the National System of Investigators. He is author of different books, articles, book chapters related to football and psychology, Speaker at different International Congresses in the area of Physical Education, Psychology and Football, and UEFA Pro football coach. He is also former employee at the High-Performance Center of the Marcet Foundation

(Specialists in Football Technification), currently coaching Tigres UANL Soccer College Team.

José Leandro Tristán-Rodríguez holds Doctorate in Science of Physical-Sports Activity and Quality of Life from the University of Murcia. He is full-time professor-researcher and Director of the School of Sports Organization, UANL; Member of the National System of Researchers (SNI) level 1; Member of the academic body "Sciences of Physical Culture and Sport" (UANL-CA-306). He was awarded the Honor to the Mexican Physical Education by the Federation International d'Education Physique (FIEP).

Angélica María Sáenz-Macana is a Ph.D. Student at the Faculty of Physical Activity and Sports Sciences of the University of Valencia. She is currently developing quantitative and qualitative research about gender and sexual diversity in Physical Education and Sport in Colombia. She is a teacher in the Secretary of Education of the District Bogotá. She participates in a research team called "Physical Activity, Education and Society" and in a critical physical education seminar called "Soca-Rel". She is a collaborator in the first Spanish research network on sport and people LGBTI+.

Pablo Ariel Scharagrodsky is Ph.D. in Social and Human Sciences. He is Research Professor at the National University of La Plata and the National University of Quilmes. He investigates subjects related to the history of education and physical education and sports in gender perspective. He has published more than 70 articles in national and international journals.

Julian Pegoraro Silvestrin holds a Master in Physical Education. He is a Ph.D. student in Human Sciences at the Federal University of Santa Catarina (UFSC), in Florianópolis, Brazil. Núcleo de Estudos e Pesquisas Educação e Sociedade Contemporânea—UFSC/UFRJ/CNPq.

LIST OF FIGURES

LIST OF TABLES

CHAPTER 1

Introduction: Shifting Research Accounts on Sexual and Gender Minority Athletes

Eric Anderson and Joaquín Piedra

INTRODUCTION

Much of the world is undergoing a liberalization of attitudes toward sexual minorities. This liberalization has occurred first and foremost within the global West; however, it has begun to be experienced within other world regions, including the global South. This chapter takes a macro, historical, perspective and examines the experiences of LGBT athletes in relation to three phases.

E. Anderson (✉)
University of Winchester, Winchester, UK

J. Piedra
Universidad de Sevilla, Sevilla, Spain
e-mail: jpiedra@us.es

J. Piedra and E. Anderson (eds.), *Lesbian, Gay, and Transgender Athletes in Latin America*, Palgrave Studies in Masculinity, Sport and Exercise, https://doi.org/10.1007/978-3-030-87375-2_1

Phase 1: The Foundation of a Socially Conservative Institution

This covers the twentieth century and is characterized by monolithic, global, homophobia, and transphobia.

Phase 2: Western Liberalization

This phase covers the first two decades of the twenty-first century and is characterized by an uneven dismantling of sporting homophobia in the global West, but entrenched transphobia, alongside continuing monolithic homophobia and transphobia throughout the rest of the world.

Phase 3: Liberal Expansion

This phase sees that homophobia is not entirely eliminated in the global West, but that it is nonetheless socially unacceptable in the majority population. This phase highlights the emergence of the beginning of the dismantling of transphobia in the West, too. This phase also sees the beginnings of liberalizing attitudes toward sexual and gender minorities in the global South; suggesting that a crack in this hegemonic homophobia has occurred.

It is our hope that understanding these three phases might help readers situate the complexity of reading chapters about the following two types of research related to LGBT athletes:

(1) the attitudes of sexual majorities (heterosexuals) and gender majorities (cisgender males and females) maintained toward LGBT people and athletes both within literature that is globally situated (geographical variance), and spans across these three phases (temporal variance).

(2) the experiences of sexual (LGB) and gender (transgender) minorities in sport, within a literature set that is both geographically variant and temporally variant.

Concerning the mixture of temporal and geographical variance, we argue that research findings from America in 1991 will no longer be valid in 2001 America. Research from 2011 America will no longer be valid in 2021. Similarly, research that was valid in America in 2021 may have some general applicability to other western regions, particularly the UK, Australia, Canada, and a few other Western European nations, but it will not be applicable to any country in the global South.

Laying out these three phases alongside geographical and temporal variance also shows a cultural lag exists between sexual minorities and gender minorities. This is because there was widespread cultural visibility of sexual minorities before there were transgender, and later, gender non-binary people. This later emergence means that the foundational years of the LGB movement were mostly exclusive of transgender people (Anderson & Travers, 2017). More so, there are far fewer transgender people to promote social visibility than there are lesbian and gay people. This visibility (contact theory) has been shown to be crucial in liberalizing attitudes of the majority (citations).

While we include bisexuals with lesbian and gay athletes in our temporal format, the reality is that this is a matter of hypothetical theorizing. This is because there has been a great invisibility of bisexual people in sexual research, even in the global West (Anderson & McCormack, 2016). There is no research specifically examining either social attitudes of athletes toward bisexual males or females, nor is there any research specifically examining the experience of bisexual athletes in sport. When they are mentioned, it is because an odd one is either caught up in research on gays or lesbians, or because a questionnaire has lumped bisexual in with attitudes toward gays and lesbians and transgender people all at once. Unfortunately, we do little to rectify the absence of bisexual people in this book. As editors, we are limited by what comes into us to publish.

This brings us to the final point. We fully recognize that there are not only variances between LGB and trans people in terms of what we are measuring (sexual vs. gender orientation) but there are often huge differences in dominant groups' attitudes toward them. Traditionally, bisexual women have received the most social favorability, followed by lesbian women, then bisexual/gay men, followed by transgender people (Anderson & McCormack, 2016). This means that it is, academically, wholly inappropriate to lump these categories of people together. Matters become even more diffuse when including intersex people, queer people, and gender non-binary people. For example, it would be poor academic practice to ask heterosexuals a question about their antipathy or sympathy for LGBT people. One might love gay men but hate transgender men.

Despite these misgivings, researchers often do this. This is because all of these categories of athletes are difficult to find. First, because LGBT people represent a small fraction of the total population. Second, because they must also choose to play sport over other cultural activities (music, arts, etc.). Third, because they must first come out in sport in order to be studied. Thus, as with studying any cultural subgroup, locating gay, lesbian, bisexual and transgender athletes is extortionary difficult: these athletes cannot be captured in meaningful numbers using population-based surveying methods or general school population studies. Instead, they must be located by more difficult recruitment means, often on an individual by individual basis. Hence, some forgiveness must come into play when a researcher decides that rather than just locating gay men in sport, they decide to capture anyone from the LGBT umbrella. Researchers are also under pressure to be inclusive of all sexual and gender minorities. Thus, they experience pressure to create surveys about LGBT people, despite the fact that participants do not view these various categories equally. This is the reality of politics and power in research.

We thus encourage readers to be mindful that it is not valid to lump their experiences together as one. Keep in mind that if a study discusses LGBT people the negative aspects will be influenced by the inclusion of transgender athletes. While we cannot always control how researchers frame their questions, and to whom they study, we can always remember that there are great variances in attitudes and life experiences between lesbians, gays, bisexual males, bisexual females, transgender males, transgender females, intersexual, queer, questioning and non-binary people, of varying temporal and geographical locations, and within varying levels of masculine to feminized sports. LGBT people are as variant as sporting spaces are.

PHASE 1: THE FOUNDATION OF A SOCIALLY CONSERVATIVE INSTITUTION

Impact of the Industrial Revolution

Our cultural, near-global, obsession with mass participation in organized, competitive teamsport can be largely traced back to the second Industrial Revolution (mid-1800s through to the early 1900s) in the global West. During this period, sturdy farmers exchanged their time-honored professions for salaried work. Families replaced their farm's rent for that of a city apartment. The allure of industry, and the better life it promised, influenced such a migration that the percentage of people living in cities rose from 25% (in 1800) to approximately 75% in 1900 (Cancian, 1987).

Just as western cities attracted people, the increasing difficulty of rural life also compelled them to leave behind their agrarian ways. This is because the same industrial technologies that brought capitalism also meant that fewer farmers were required to produce the necessary crops to feed a growing population. With production capacity rising, and crop prices falling, families were not only drawn to cities by the allure of a stable wage and the possibility of class mobility; they were also repelled by an increasingly difficult agrarian labor market and an inability to own land.

For all the manifestations of physical horror that was factory life (before labor laws), there were many advantages, too. Related to the establishment of mass participation in western sport, the regularity of work meant that between blows of the factory whistle, there was time for men to play. The concept of leisure, once reserved for the wealthy, thus spread to the working class during this period (Rigauer, 1981). It is the sociocultural impact of this great migration that is central to the development of men's sport in Western cultures.

Somewhat predictably, it was also around this time that the organization, codification, and regulation of most dominant sports—especially contact teamsports—occurred in Anglo-American cultures. Soccer, for example, formally codified in 1863, when there was a necessity to unify several different codes of the game. Other popular teamsports also emerged around this time, too, including baseball (1840s), rugby union (1840s), American football (1860s), basketball (1890s), and rugby league (1890s).

While sport maintained little cultural value prior to the Industrial Revolution, by the second decade of the next century these sentiments had been reversed (Miracle & Rees, 1994). Sport gave boys something to do after school. It helped socialize them into the values necessary to be successful in this new economy, to instill the qualities of discipline and obedience, and to honor the hard work that was necessary in the dangerous occupations of industrial labor and mining (Rigauer, 1981). Accordingly, workers needed to sacrifice both their time and their health, for the sake of making the wage they needed to support their dependent families.

In sport, young boys were socialized into this value of sacrifice (for team), so that they would later sacrifice health and well-being for family at work. Most important to the bourgeois ruling class, however, workers needed to be obedient to authority. Sport taught boys this docility. Accordingly, organized competitive teamsport was funded by those who maintained control of the reproduction of material goods. Children's play was forced off the streets (spontaneous street-playing activities were banned) and into parks and playgrounds, where they were supervised and structured in their "play." Just as they are today, organized youth sport was financially backed by business, in the form of "sponsors." Today, as part of a compulsory state-run education, they are often backed by the state. This is an economical way of assuring a docile and productive labor force.

These environments necessitated that men be tough and unemotional. Men grew more instrumental not only in their labor and purpose, but in their personalities, too. Fathers left for work early, often returning home once their sons had gone to bed. Because teaching children was considered "women's work," boys spent much of their days (at school and home) surrounded by women. Here, they were thought to be deprived of the masculine vapors supposedly necessary to masculinize them. It was thus feared that men were also becoming "soft," that society itself was becoming feminized—a by-product of industrialization. The stage was set for a "crisis of masculinity" (Filene, 1975).

Simultaneous to this, however, was the first wave of women's political independence (Hargreaves, 1986). The city provided a density of women that made activism more accessible. Smith-Rosenberg (1985) suggests that men felt threatened by the political and social advancements of women at the time; they were losing their patriarchal power. The antidote to the rise of women's agency largely came through sport. But a much under-theorized influence on the development and promotion of sport comes through the changing understanding of sexuality during the Industrial Revolution.

This is perhaps most salient through Sigmund Freud's (1905) work, *Three Essays on the Theory of Sexuality*. Here, Freud theorized that sexuality was not innate, but instead that childhood experiences constructed men to become heterosexual or homosexual—what he called "inversion." Freud essentially argued that heterosexuality was a process of gendered wrongdoing, particularly through the absence of a father figure and an over-domineering mother. He wrote: "The presence of both parents plays an important part. The absence of a strong." As a consequence of Freud's work, however, came a moral panic among Victorian-thinking British and American cultures. To them, it seemed that because industrialization pulled fathers away from their families for large periods of time—while they were out at work—it had created a social system "designed" to make boys gay. At this time, then, what it meant to "be a man" was positioned as opposite to homosexuality. Indeed, being masculine entailed being the opposite of the softness attributed to gay men. According to Kimmel (1994), heterosexuality grew further predicated in avoidance of anything coded as vaguely feminine. To be a man in the twentieth century was, therefore, to be unlike a woman. In this environment, organized, competitive, and violent sports were thrust upon boys.

Sport as a Masculine Cure-All

In this exclusive atmosphere, sport became associated with the political project to reverse the feminizing and homosexualizing trends of boys growing up without father figures. Sport and those who coached it were responsible for with shaping boys into heterosexual, masculine men. Accordingly, a rapid rise and expansion of organized sport was utilized as a homosocial institution principally aimed to counter men's fears of feminism and homosexuality.

This period also saw organized sport being co-opted by adults (Guttmann, 1978). Prior to the 1890s sporting matches were controlled by students—they were coached by students, organized and played all by and for students. However, with new reasons for valuing sport, coaches were paid to manage sport. It was also during this time that recreational sport became enveloped by school systems (particularly in the US), a relationship that continues today. These mirrors and trains youth to cooperate with bureaucratic structures so evident in contemporary Anglo-American societies. Accordingly, these processes are how a once unimportant social institution suddenly found merit and purpose, by those in power.

Modern sport was therefore born out of the turn of the twentieth-century notion that it could help prevent male youth from possessing characteristics associated with femininity. It was designed to compel boys to reject all but a narrow definition of masculinity: one that created good industrial workers, soldiers, Christians, and consumers. The construction of sport as a masculine and homophobic enterprise was both deliberate and political.

The commercial and cultural values of sport become a global phenomenon as the decades of the twentieth century grew. We do not claim that all cultures took up sport for the same reasons as it emerged in the global West, but there is no denying that by the end of the twentieth century sport was established as global institution of conservative values.

The whole process of colonization, as well as media globalization afterward, helped the spread of conservative values in the global South during the nineteenth and twentieth centuries.

Experiencing Sport as a Gay or Lesbian Athlete in the Twentieth Century

Researchers who have examined the issue of same-sex attracted males in sport within the twentieth century, and bleeding into the twenty-first, concur that that organized sports were, monolithically, a highly homophobic institution (Hekma, 1998; Pronger, 1992; Wolf-Wendel et al., 2001). Drawing on his study of heterosexual males in the late 1970s, Messner (1992, p. 34) wrote, "The extent of homophobia in the sports world is staggering. Boys (in sports) learn early that to be gay, to be suspected of being gay, or even to be unable to prove one's heterosexual status is not acceptable." Even researching community sport athletes in the late 1990s, Hekma (1998, p. 2) found that gay men in Netherlands "...who are seen as queer and effeminate are granted no space whatsoever in what is generally considered to be a masculine preserve and a macho enterprise." And Pronger (1992, p. 26) noted of Canadian gay men at the time that, "Many of the (gay) men I interviewed said they were uncomfortable with team sports...orthodox masculinity is usually an important subtext if not the leitmotif" in team sports.

The hostility toward sexual minorities within this institution stems from its twentieth-century origins (Anderson, 2005). Sports have been described as a place in which hegemonic masculinity is reproduced and defined, as an athlete represents the ideal of what it means to be a man, a definition which contrasts what it means to be feminine and/or gay (Connell, 1995). And as women have increasingly gained access to once masculine-dominated institutions throughout the latter decades of the twentieth century, some argue that sports became contested terrain in which men tried to validate masculine privilege through their ability to physically outperform women, thus symbolically dominating women (Burton-Nelson, 1994).

Thus, the historically socially conservative nature of sport impacted upon female athletes as well. Despite the cultural association of female athleticism with same-sex attraction, twentieth-century homophobia has also been described as rife within female sport. Sociologists examining the issue of lesbians in sport during the 1980s and 1990s agreed that organized team sports were normally characterized as highly homophobic organizational cultures (Griffin, 1998; Lenskyj, 1986; Sykes, 1998; Veri, 1999).

We think it is therefore almost entirely incontrovertible, that sport was designed for the promotion of heterosexual, masculine males first, was then extended to females in the later decades of the twentieth century. However, hostility toward LGB athletes, and presumably transgender athletes (if it had been studied), was monolithic across all cultures up until perhaps the last few years of the twentieth century, and their bleeding into the twenty-first. Here we began to see a liberalization of broader attitudes, which lagged behind (at first) in sport, toward sexual minorities.

Phase 2: Western Liberalization

Over the past three decades, there has been a rapid increase in liberal attitudes toward sexual minorities in the West (Pew, 2020). The United States as an exemplar of this shift (Loftus, 2001). There is an overwhelming body of quantitative and qualitative evidence that suggests that cultural homophobia began to decrease in 1993 and has rapidly decreased ever since (e.g., Anderson, 2009; Baunach, 2012). Keleher and Smith (2012, p. 1324) show that *all* demographic groups have become more tolerant and, importantly, that they became more tolerant at the same rate; arguing that, "we are witnessing a sweeping change in attitudes toward lesbians and gay men." Studies continue to show this progression toward inclusivity (Twenge et al., 2016).

Decreasing homophobia also encapsulates decreasing biphobia (Anderson & McCormack 2016; Anderson et al., 2015, 2016a, 2016b). Not only has this made bisexuality more legitimate, but it has rapidly expanded the sexual behaviors available to heterosexual males to be inclusive of same-sex activities (Branfman et al., 2018). This liberalization has led to a number of policy changes, including marriage equality, and in many conic cultural moments for increased citizenship status for sexual minorities (Ofosu et al., 2019).

Significant to social theory on masculinity, a substantial and growing body of newer work eschews viewing boys as desiring to be homophobic in order to be masculine, the way Connell (1995) theorized. Instead, many scholars of masculinity have turned to a more nuanced perspective on the western construction of masculinity that sees a decrease of cultural homophobia also impacting upon a shift of males desiring to not be seen as acting in hyper-masculine ways. Anderson proffers, Inclusive Masculinity Theory (2009) to explain the relationship, and shift, between attitudes toward gay men and heterosexual masculinities. You will thus see several authors utilizing this theory in this book.

This liberalization trend is domain to more than just sport. In 2021, Gallup showed that, for the first time in American history, less than half (47%) of adult Americans were affiliated with a church, synagogue, or mosque. This represents more than a 20-point decline since the turn of the twenty-first century; meaning that religious affiliation—another bastion of social conservativism—is declining at about a percent a year.

There is literature examining this shift in American fraternities. Rankin et al. (2013) conduct a cohort analysis to show that, among 337 self-identified gay and bisexual fraternity members, those who joined the fraternity in the year since 2000 have a more positive experience overall as fraternity members than did the participants who joined at any time prior.

It also is found within the armed services. There has been a cohort analysis examining the willingness of LGBT service people to come out within the military setting; unsurprisingly finding a shift here, too (Evans et al., 2019).

Finally, there is a body of research showing improved attitudinal disposition among heterosexual athletes toward LGBT athletes (Cunningham & Pickett, 2018); as well as several qualitative investigations showing that gay (Anderson, 2005) and lesbian (Anderson et al., 2016a, 2016b) athletes experience acceptance within team culture. What is missing from this body of research however—and the first purpose of this research—is a large-scale survey of LGBT athlete experiences in American Sport.

Experiencing Sport as a Western Gay or Lesbian Athlete in the Twenty-First Century

The turn of the twenty-first century, however, marks a change for research examining LGBT athletes, and a crack to the monolithic findings of overt intolerance in the West. The relevant research comes from two locus of study. First, research examining the attitudes of heterosexual athletes toward having an LGBT teammate; and second, research on the experiences of LGBT athletes within sport.

There are a few survey studies that examine heterosexual athletes' attitudes toward having a lesbian, bisexual, or gay teammate. Cunningham and Pickett (2018) use two identical investigations of attitudinal prejudice toward LGBT American athletes in 2007 and 2014, to show a social upgrading of heterosexual disposition toward lesbian, gay, and bisexual athletes between these two periods. Also consistent with our stage model, his research showed less acceptance of transgender people in sport.

Similarly, Anderson uses identical qualitative studies (2002 and 2011), each with a sampling of 28 gay male athletes, to show improved gay male experiences in sport, as well as increased ease in finding athletes to study.

More so, a longitudinal study from the UK (Bush et al., 2012) showed improving yearly attitudes among 18-year-old university athletes in England and, at the same time, using the same Attitudes Toward Gays and Lesbians Scale (Herek & McLemore, 1998), an equivalent American study found more homophobia among 391 American undergraduate athletes in the Midwest; 19% expressed homophobic sentiment toward sexual minorities (Anderson & Mowatt, 2013).

Finally, in a 2010 sample of Division I and III male university athletes ($n = 397$), they were asked how they would or do treat a teammate they think or know is gay or bisexual. Approximately 66 percent ($n = 254$) of male athletes who answered the question reported they would or do accept a gay or bisexual teammate, while 28 percent ($n = 110$) reported they would/do "reject" a gay/bisexual teammate, and another 6 percent ($n = 24$) say that they do or would "harass" a gay or bisexual teammate. The sample was near evenly split between team and individual sport athletes, yet of the 110 rejecting male athletes, sixty-eight were football players; thus these findings located higher rates of homophobia among team sport athletes (Southall et al., 2009).

Concerning whether these liberalizing attitudes transition into improved experiences for LGB athletes, something of a methodological paradox does materialize. On the one hand, quantitative work shows a modest degree of discrimination, while the qualitative work does not.

Examining the experiences of sexual minorities in sport with survey methods, Pariera et al. (2021) found 20% of their $N = 77$ participants reported being treated unfairly based on their sexual orientation and 30% report having at least once been harassed though homophobic discourse. The dominant form of this discrimination concerned feeling that they could not talk openly about their sexuality.

The world's largest quantitative study of LGBT people and their experiences of sport comes from Hartmann-Tews et al. (2020), and their investigation into European LGBT people. They boost of a huge sample size, 5524, of which 2154 indicated that within the last year they had played competitive 28.5% or high-performance sport (10.5%). This leaves 840 competitive athletes surveyed for their experiences in sport.

This is quite a large number of people involved with sport, across Europe: which has vastly different attitudes toward LGBT people from nation to nation. Their results show that 49% of those athletes heard at least one homophobic or transphobic comment within the last 12 months. This is indicated by hearing one term, by one player, on any team or in any location, toward anyone (not just the participant) in any context. So, this is not a sample of frequency or percent of athletes who use this form of terminology. This means that over half of the athletes surveyed have experienced no such language in the past year.

Perhaps more significant, these researchers report that 11.7% of their sample had a bad personal experience. However, the authors were clear to identify that not all people under the LGBT+ umbrella suffered equally. They write "The most striking differences can be found between non-cisgender and cisgender respondents, as non-cisgender respondents show a three times higher share (27.3%) of negative personal experiences. This effect consistently occurs in all settings and types of sports." (p. 13). With regard to sexual orientation, respondents who indicated having a SO other than gay, lesbian, or bisexual (19.3%) have had the most homo-/transnegative experiences. Given the sample had a high rate of transgender and gender non-binary people, at 19.1%, this means that the 11.7% headline figure is disproportionally weighted down by transphobia, and antipathy toward those with sexual orientations that are not gay, lesbian, or bi.

There are some limitations and drawbacks to this study. First, we do not know what percent of these athletes may have been out of the closet on their teams. The researchers did not ask. This is important because homophobic antipathy decreases after a gay athlete comes out (Anderson, 2005). Second, we do not know much about the variance by age-cohort. Participants were aged up until 78 years old. Given that there is a cohort effect at play with attitudes toward sexual and gender minorities more fully (Baunach, 2012), it is likely that poorer experiences are associated with older age groups.

Another large scale, but limited study, comes from Denison et al. (2021), which conducted research in 2014. This research shows that, among openly gay LGBT participants gathered from an online survey of six nations (USA, UK, Australia, New Zealand, Ireland, and Canada) in 2013, 442 reported having ever been out to some or all teammates. While the study found that (57.7%, $N = 109$) of those who came out to all; and (46.6%; $N = 118$) of those who came out to some, reported they had been the target of homophobic discourse, the study has serious flaws and limitations. First, it was retrospective in account, without age controls, so that even those who came out decades ago were included in the results. Second, there were not jokesters' controls. Third, there were no controls for participants from school teams versus community or professional levels of sports. Still, this research backs up the Hartmann-Tews et al. (2020), in showing that the primary problem that LGBT athletes have in sport concerns homophobic discourse.

A few years later (White et al., 2020) examined almost the same number of participants, but exclusively focused on the written narratives of openly gay male athletes who wrote about their coming out stories on the Web site, Outsports.com. Unlike historical account of Denison et al. (2021) work, they only examined athletes who had come out since 2015. They show that prior to coming out, many of the $N = 60$ athletes felt the need to adopt an identity predicated on masculine stereotypes, thus distancing themselves from homosexuality. Upon coming out to teammates, however, 58 of these athletes experienced acceptance and inclusivity which, in turn, led to improved health and well-being. These 60 accounts are affirmed by interview research $N = 28$ (Anderson, 2011), showing American gay male teamsport athletes thriving.

We highlight that academic research is not what likely fuels the cultural conception of homophobia in sport. Instead, we argue that Americans are influenced into the disposition of ongoing and extreme sporting homophobia because of the near-total absence of professional gay males in the professional ranks of sport. While there exist approximately 3500 professional team sport positions between the North American baseball, basketball, football, and hockey leagues, with a rotation of that roster in less than three years, there are no athletes who are currently playing out of the closet in any of these professional sports, and only a handful who have ever come out. This great absence is rife for hypothesizing homophobia as the leading factor (Anderson et al., 2016a, 2016b). The situation might easily lead to the cultural conception that, despite liberalizing attitudes toward sexual minorities across American society, sport remains unaltered in its treatment of sexual minority athletes. We note that the same affect may be at play in the global South.

We leave this section by highlighting the primary findings. First, it appears that whereas homophobia was culturally endorsed, and homosexuality culturally stigmatized in the twentieth century (across all geographical domains), in the twenty-first century we see that it is now homophobia which is no longer socially acceptable in the West. Despite this, there has yet to be published research definitively proving that LGB (and T) athletes experience this acceptance monolithically, or near-so.

This is about to change. In the early months of 2021, Professor Eric Anderson partnered up with Cyd Zeigler, of the American-based Web site devoted specifically to LGBT athletes in sport. They devised and launched a survey, using dozens of others to help them locate LGBT people who have or currently play openly in sport as an American or Canadian (only) LGBT athlete, in high school and/or college (university) sports. While the survey is still active at the time of this writing (and will not be at the time of publication), a sneak preview seems fair.

Thus far, this group of scholars have collected over 1000 surveys (with jokesters controls, repeated measures controls, and one that accounts for temporal variance so that we know what year they came out). We show a participant demographic in which the far majority have come out around 2015 or later; in which gay males are about 62% of the population (majority) and trans athletes the minority, at about 3% of the population. We show that when you aggregate the high school and university responses and aggregate all the LGB and T people into one figure, only 3% report having a "bad" or "very bad" experience (about evenly split 1.5% each). Conversely, about 7% report having a neutral experience, and the rest a good, very good experience (60%) and about 30% report having a near-perfect experience on their team.

PHASE 3: LIBERAL EXPANSION OUTSIDE THE GLOBAL WEST

The story of our phase model is thus far briefly: (1) Organized competitive team sports emerged in the global West as a social institution with political purpose to masculinize and heterosexualize boys and men. (2) Sport took on other purposes throughout the twentieth century, in the West, and in the latter decades women's participation grew. (3) By the end of the twentieth sport participation for youth was a global product. (4) Here it retained its conservative, and thus homophobic and trans-phobic roots. (5) However, the twenty-first century saw a liberalizing of social attitudes and improving experiences of sexual minorities, including in sport. (6) Today, while homophobia still exists in the West, it is socially stigmatized, and the experience of LGB athletes is near-monolithically good. Transgender athletes remain the area of focus for improvement in the West, today.

The next phase in this story concerns the near-global expansion of the liberalization of attitudes toward sexual minorities outside of the West: liberal expansion. This does not mean that homophobia is gone in all countries—far from it. It simply indicates that, on a global scale, attitudes toward LGBT people are on the whole, improving (Pew, 2020).

This improvement exists in most every country studied, apart from a few (Greece, Lebanon, Russia). In some of those countries the improvement is from practically no support to just some. For example, between 2013 and 2019 Tunisia moved from 2 to 9 percent saying homosexuality should be accepted in society, and in Nigeria it's from 1 to 7. Sweden comes in at 94 and the Netherlands at 92.

Unique to this episodic phase is the emergence and rapid adoption of transgender and other sexual (asexual, bisexual, pansexual, demisexual) minorities, as well as sexual minorities (intersex) and gender minorities (queer, gender non-binary). Today, we often lump these varying sexual and gender minorities under a LGBT+ categorical system (with its inherent faults and limitations).

This is where this book finds its place in the history of LGBT research in sport. It represents the first book-length manuscript examining the relationship between sexual and gender minority athletes in the global South.

THE CONTENT OF THIS BOOK

We highlight here that just like there is attitudinal variance in the Anglo-American and other Western European countries that we collectively describe as the West, there is equal variance or greater in the global South. This book details research from Spanish and Portuguese speaking countries that do not view homosexuality equally.

Pew research shows, for example, that as of 2019, by the same question of whether homosexuality should be socially accepted, 72% of Americans and 86% of British people agree. Argentina comes in higher than the States, at 76% and Mexico at 69%. Spain beats all of them, at 89%. So, it is not an appropriate lens to view "the West" as necessarily leading the way here: Spain had gay marriage 11 years before America.

But there does seem to be a difference in the treatment of LGBT athletes between the English and Spanish or Portuguese speaking countries. The reasons for this are not immediately clear. We know that, in the States, attitudes toward homosexuality are much more positive among youth than the elderly (Keleher and Smith, 2012). Perhaps this same affect is not in play in Spain. This might be why Piedra et al. (2017) find more inclusive masculinities among British adolescents than Spanish. The role of religion and other cultural elements complicate matters.

In short, sport may be differently conservative in some countries with liberal attitudes than other countries with liberal attitudes. We just don't know. It highlights, however, that sport can still be a conservative bastion, even within liberalized nations.

We are, however, very pleased to provide to you ten chapters examining a breadth of topics from this to that in this book. In order to know and better understand how these countries and cultures embrace sexual diversity in sport, the book is structured in three sections.

The first chapter in the initial section, signed by Spanish researchers Joan Miró and Joaquín Piedra, analyzes the historical evolution of LGBT sports clubs in both Spain and Latin America. This text justifies and defends the existence of LGBT sports clubs in the sports scene as a means to normalize and make visible the realities of this community. It also describes the evolution of the clubs created in Latin America, the current scenario for these organizations, as well as future problems. Knowing the path followed by sports organizations in our culture will allow us to establish similarities with associations and clubs created in other cultures, as well as to contrast the differences between them. Works such as those by Jarvis (2015) or Elling and Janssens (2009) on the role of LGBT clubs as scenarios for negotiation and visibilization are the basis for defending the presence of these spaces of freedom. However, until now, no attention has been focused on the specific situation of clubs in Spain and Latin America.

In the second chapter of the first section of the book, Vinnicius Laurindo and Mariana Zuaneti Martins review the scientific production in

Brazil on LGBT issues in sport. This review shows an increasing visibility in some themes or areas, as in the case of lesbians in soccer or gay men in volleyball. However, other research themes remain taboo in this country. Likewise, the authors point out the importance of intersecting studies on sexual diversity with other variables of great importance in their country, such as class and race. Some recent events in Brazil are opening up the debate on issues that have not been explored until now, such as transgender athletes. This path in the academic sphere, of progressive openness to studies on homophobia or transphobia, is also taking place in other cultures, such as Spain. It is precisely this book that will allow us to find out what degree of academic interest these issues are gaining in different countries.

In the last chapter of the section, Joaquín Piedra, Rafael García-Pérez, and Alex Channon present the idea of pseudo-inclusivity developed from Anderson's Inclusive Masculinity Theory (2009). This new stage suggested by authors previously (Piedra et al., 2017) is contextualized in Spain and Mexico societies. Mexican and Spanish culture are assessed theoretically as incomplete or under construction inclusive societies. Differences and similarities are analyzed among both countries. Yet, future research must be done in order to go through this study.

The second section of the book shows different visions that exist in Latin American countries. As we have pointed out before, diversity, miscegenation, and religion are some of the features of Latin culture. Thus, each country, each region, will have created a way of developing physical activity and sport, as well as a way of looking at people's sexual and gender identity. This is why each of these chapters deals with the concrete and particular vision of sport, explained in light of traditions, customs, and practices of a given context.

The first of these realities is embodied in British researcher George Jennings' anthropological study of the Mexican martial art of Xilam. The existence of an entire culture, dating back to pre-Columbian times, is explained in detail and in first person by an anthropologist who is an expert in martial arts. The sexual and gender vision of this philosophy and art is still present, and permeates the understanding of the reality of its practitioners. This chapter undertakes an interesting journey to make known a minority reality even within Mexican culture itself. Thus, it tries to shed light on the general through the explanation of the particular, creating a connection between the sporting, the philosophical and even the ethnic. There is published work on sexuality in other martial disciplines in Europe (Channon & Matthews, 2015) or Asia (Expósito-Barea, 2012), but no papers on Latin American contexts.

The second chapter of this section focuses on Mexican athletes' attitudes toward sexual diversity into sport. Findings of this research in the field of psychology show barriers to LGBT participation in Mexican sport. Through a quantitative study, Oswaldo Ceballos and his colleagues explain that, among men observed, there is higher discrimination and discomfort for sexual orientations other than heterosexual. This data shed light on differences and similarities among Mexican sport context and other cultures more studied.

With regard to Brazilian culture, a case study of the Brazilian soccer player, Richarlyson, by researcher Jorge Knijnik is presented. This chapter discusses the role of football in the configuration of masculinities in Brazil. The author presents the intriguing, vexing, wonderful, and horrible life of a man who decided to live his ambiguous masculinity openly. Brazilian football has shown different ways to assault and insult this different lifestyle. But this story has provoked a real crack on the once monolithic space of orthodox masculinity in South America.

In the last chapter in this section, we present a new review about what has published on sexual orientation and gender identity in Colombian sport. Angélica Sáenz-Macana and her colleagues analyze eight documents, including grey literature, where using different methodological approaching. This chapter represents the first attempt in Colombia to explore the policy and practice of LGBT people and sport participation. Researchers examined the types of sport LGBT people are engaged with, the discrimination and support experienced by them. Findings show attention from rulers and policymakers, as well as the scarcity of data available to reconstruct the practice of LGBT sport participation.

The last section of the book continues to address the reality and the particular situation of the transgender community in Latin America. Within sport, the situation of this minority group is still mostly unknown: despite the studies carried out with gays and lesbians, there are few works that focus their analysis on this group (Lucas-Carr & Krane, 2011). Furthermore, the binary configuration of competitive sport throughout its history (male and female competition) makes it difficult to find an easy solution to this issue. The confusion and lack of knowledge leads certain people and institutions to reproduce discriminatory actions toward them (Caudwell, 2014; Hargie et al., 2017).

In order to better understand the reality of this group in contexts other than those already studied (English speaking countries), we first present the work of Julian Silvestrin and Alexandre Fernandez Vaz. These researchers analyze the emergence of four trans masculine football teams in Brazil, where football is part of configuration of national identity. Findings points out that trans football player are changing football as a scenario for the identification and construction of trans masculinities. Nevertheless, it is still perceived a permanent negotiation between gender and sports performances by the individuals involved in the practice. This chapter displays an interesting research theme which shows new ways to challenge heteronormativity, merely through the presence of trans bodies in football fields.

In the final chapter of the section, Argentine researchers Magalí Pérez-Riedel and Pablo Scharagrodsky address the situation of students and teachers in an Argentinean school created as an inclusive space for trans people. Through interviews with students and teachers at this school, they show the vision and experiences of this group when it comes to doing physical activity, as well as the challenges and contradictions they have to face during sport.

These 12 chapters help us address the aims of the book: To make concrete the studies already carried out in other cultures to the reality and context of Spanish and Portuguese speaking countries. The particularities of each culture mean that the explanations and arguments may vary from one part of the continent to another. We hope to offer the reader an interesting and easy to read document.

References

Anderson, E. (2011). Updating the outcome: Gay athletes, straight teams, and coming out in educationally based sport teams. *Gender & Society, 25*(2), 250–268.

Anderson, A. R., & Mowatt, R. A. (2013). Heterosexism in campus recreational club sports: An exploratory investigation into attitudes toward gay men and lesbians. *Recreational Sports Journal, 37*(2), 106–122.

Anderson, E. (2002). Openly gay athletes: Contesting hegemonic masculinity in a homophobic environment. *Gender & Society, 16*(6), 860–877. https://doi.org/10.1177/089124302237892

Anderson, E. (2005). *In the game: Gay athletes and the cult of masculinity*. State University of New York Press.

Anderson, E. (2009). *Inclusive masculinity the changing nature of masculinities*. Routledge.

Anderson, E., & McCormack, M. (2016). *The changing dynamics of bisexual men's lives*. Springer.

Anderson, E., Magrath, R., & Bullingham, R. (2016a). *Out in sport*. Routledge.

Anderson, E., McCormack, M., & Ripley, M. (2016b). Sixth form girls and bisexual burden. *Journal of Gender Studies, 25*(1), 24–34. https://doi.org/10.1080/09589236.2013.877383

Anderson, E., Scoats, R., & McCormack, M. (2015). Metropolitan bisexual men's relationships: Evidence of a cohort effect. *Journal of Bisexuality, 15*(1), 21–39. https://doi.org/10.1080/15299716.2014.994055

Anderson, E., & Travers, A. (Eds.). (2017). *Transgender athletes in competitive sport*. Taylor & Francis.

Baunach, D. M. (2012). Changing same-sex marriage attitudes in America from 1988 through 2010. *Public Opinion Quarterly, 76*(2), 364–378. https://doi.org/10.1093/poq/nfs022

Branfman, J., Stiritz, S., & Anderson, E. (2018). Relaxing the straight male anus: Decreasing homohysteria around anal eroticism. *Sexualities, 21*(1–2), 109–127.

Burton-Nelson, M. (1994). *The stronger women get, the more men love football*. Avon Books.

Bush, A., Anderson, E., & Carr, S. (2012). The declining existence of men's homophobia in British sport. *Journal for the Study of Sports and Athletes in Education, 6*(1), 107–120. https://doi.org/10.1179/ssa.2012.6.1.107

Cancian, F. M. (1987). *Love in America: Gender and self-development*. Cambridge University Press.

Caudwell, J. (2014). [Transgender] young men: Gendered subjectivities and the physically active body. *Sport, Education and Society, 19*(4), 398–414. https://doi.org/10.1080/13573322.2012.672320

Channon, A., & Matthews, C. R. (2015). "It is what it is": Masculinity, homosexuality, and inclusive discourse in mixed martial arts. *Journal of Homosexuality, 62*(7), 936–956. https://doi.org/10.1080/00918369.2015.1008280

Connell, R. W. (1995). *Masculinities*. Berkeley.

Cunningham, G. B., & Pickett, A. C. (2018). Trans prejudice in sport: Differences from LGB prejudice, the influence of gender, and changes over time. *Sex Roles, 78*(3), 220–227. https://doi.org/10.1007/s11199-017-0791-6

Denison, E., Bevan, N., & Jeanes, R. (2021). Reviewing evidence of LGBTQ+ discrimination and exclusion in sport. *Sport Management Review*. https://doi.org/10.1016/j.smr.2020.09.003

Elling, A., & Janssens, J. (2009). Sexuality as a structural principle in sport participation. Negotiating sports spaces. *International Review for the Sociology of Sport, 44*(1), 71–89. https://doi.org/10.1177/1012690209102639

Evans, W. R., Bliss, S. J., Rincon, C. M., Johnston, S. L., Bhakta, J. P., Webb-Murphy, J. A. et al. (2019). Military service members' satisfaction with outness: Implications for mental health', *Armed Forces & Society*, *45*(1), 140–154.https://doi.org/10.1177/0095327X17751111

Expósito-Barea, M. (2012). From the Iron to the Lady: The "kathoey" phenomenon in Thai cinema. *Sesión No Numerada: Revista De Letras y Ficción Audiovisual*, *2*, 190–202.

Filene, P. G. (1975). *Him/her/self: Sex roles in modern America*. Johns Hopkins University Press.

Gallup (2021). https://news.gallup.com/poll/341963/church-membership-falls-below-majority-first-time.aspx. Retrieved at March 29, 2021.

Griffin, P. (1998). *Strong women, deep closets*. Human Kinetics.

Guttmann, A. (1978). *From ritual to record: The nature of modern sports*. Columbia University Press.

Hargie, O., Mitchell, D., & Somerville, I. (2017). 'People have a knack of making you feel excluded if they catch on to your difference': Transgender experiences of exclusion in sport. *International Review for the Sociology of Sport*, *52*(2), 223–239. https://doi.org/10.1177/1012690215583283

Hargreaves, J. (1986). *Sport, power and culture: A social and historical analysis of popular sports in britain*. Polity.

Hartmann-Tews, I., Menzel, T., & Braumüller, B. (2020). Homo-and transneg-ativity in sport in Europe: Experiences of LGBT+ individuals in various sport settings. *International Review for the Sociology of Sport*, https://doi.org/10.1177/1012690220968108

Hekma, G. (1998). "As Long as They Don't Make an Issue of It...": Gay men and lesbians in organised sports in the Netherlands. *Journal of Homosexuality*, *35*(1), 1–23. https://doi.org/10.1300/J082v35n01_01

Herek, G. M., & McLemore, K. A. (1998). Attitudes toward lesbians and gay men scale. *Handbook of sexuality-related measures*, 392–394.

Jarvis, N. (2015). The inclusive masculinities of heterosexual men within UK gay sport clubs. *International Review for the Sociology of Sport*, *50*(3), 283–300. https://doi.org/10.1177/1012690213482481

Keleher, A., & Smith, E. R. (2012). Growing support for gay and lesbian equality since 1990. *Journal of Homosexuality*, *59*(9), 1307–1326. https://doi.org/10.1080/00918369.2012.720540

Kimmel, M. S. (1994). Masculinity as homophobia: Fear, shame, and silence in the construction of gender identity. In H. Brod & M. Kaufman (Eds.), *Theorizing Masculinities* (pp. 223–242). Sage.

Lenskyj, H. J. (1986). *Out of Bounds: Women*. Women's Press.

Loftus, J. (2001). America's liberalization in attitudes towards homosexuality, 1973 to 1998. *American Sociological Review*, *66*(5), 762–782. https://doi.org/10.2307/3088957

Lucas-Carr, C. B., & Krane, V. (2011). What Is the T in LGBT? Supporting Transgender Athletes Through Sport Psychology. *The Sport Psychologist*, *25*(4), 532–548. https://doi.org/10.1123/tsp.25.4.532

Messner, M. A. (1992). When bodies are weapons. *Peace Review, 4*(3), 28–31.

Miracle, A. W., & Rees, C. R. (1994). *Lesson of the locker room: The myth of school sports.* Prometheus.

Ofosu, E. K., Chambers, M. K., Chen, J. M., & Hehman, E. (2019). Same-sex marriage legalization associated with reduced implicit and explicit antigay bias. *Proceedings of the National Academy of Sciences, 116*(18), 8846–8851.

Pariera, K., Brody, E., & Scott, D. T. (2021). Now that they're out: experiences of college athletics teams with openly LGBTQ players. *Journal of Homosexuality, 68*(5), 733–751. https://doi.org/10.1080/00918369.2019.1661727

Pew. (2020, January 25). https://www.pewresearch.org/global/2020/06/25/global-divide-on-homosexuality-persists/.

Piedra, J., García-Pérez, R., & Channon, A. (2017). Between homohysteria and inclusivity: Tolerance towards sexual diversity in sport. *Sexuality & Culture, 21*(4), 1018–1039. https://doi.org/10.1007/s12119-017-9434-x

Pronger, B. (1992). *The arena of masculinity: Sports, homosexuality, and the meaning of sex.* Macmillan.

Rankin, S. R., Hesp, G. A., & Weber, G. N. (2013). Experiences and perceptions of gay and bisexual fraternity members from 1960 to 2007: A cohort analysis. *Journal of College Student Development, 54*(6), 570–590. https:// doi.org/ https://doi.org/10.1353/csd.2013.0091

Rigauer, B. (1981). *Sport and Work.* Columbia University Press.

Smith-Rosenberg, C. (1985). *Disorderly conduct: Visions of gender in Victorian America.* Oxford University Press.

Southall, R. M., Nagel, M. S., Anderson, E., Polite, F. G., & Southall, C. (2009). An investigation of male college athletes' attitudes toward sexual-orientation. *Journal of Issues in Intercollegiate Athletics, Special Issue,* 62–77.

Sykes, H. (1998). Turning the closets inside out: Towards a queer-feminist theory in women's physical education. *Sociology of Sport Journal, 15*(2), 154–173. https://doi.org/10.1123/ssj.15.2.154

Twenge, J. M., Ryne, A. S., & Wells, B. (2016). Changes in american adults' reported same-sex sexual experiences and attitudes, 1973–2014. *Archives of Sexual Behaviour, 45*(7), 1713–1730. https://doi.org/10.1007/s10508-016-0769-4

Veri, M. J. (1999). Homophobic discourse surrounding the female athlete. *Quest, 51*(4), 355–368. https://doi.org/10.1080/00336297.1999.10491691

White, A. J., Magrath, R., & Emilio Morales, L. (2020). Gay male athletes' coming-out stories on Outsports.com. *International Review for the Sociology of Sport.* https://doi.org/10.1177/1012690220969355

Wolf-Wendel, L., Toma, D., & Morphew, C. (2001). How much difference is too much difference? Perceptions of gay men and lesbians in intercollegiate athletics. *Journal of College Student Development, 42*(5), 465–479.

PART I

Historical and Sociological Perspectives

CHAPTER 2

LGBT Sport Clubs: Origin and Historical Changes in Spain and Latin America

Joan Miró and Joaquín Piedra

WHY ARE LGBT SPORTS CLUBS NECESSARY?

This is the first question asked to members of LGBT sport clubs and the one which generates more controversy. This is because these types of sport clubs are considered, by certain people, as a form of social segregation (locking themselves in a ghetto) instead of being integrated into mainstream sport clubs. From our perspective however, just asking this question provides an example of the operation of homophobia in society. This is because the same questions are not frequently asked of other identity-based sport clubs. For example, there exists clubs based on occupation (World Police and Fire Games), religion (Celtic Glasgow—Catholics vs Glasgow Rangers—Protestants), socio-economic class (River

J. Miró
Panteres Grogues LGTBI+ Club, Barcelona, Spain

J. Piedra (✉)
Universidad de Sevilla, Sevilla, Spain
e-mail: jpiedra@us.es

© The Author(s), under exclusive license to Springer Nature   25
Switzerland AG 2021
J. Piedra and E. Anderson (eds.), *Lesbian, Gay, and Transgender Athletes in Latin America*, Palgrave Studies in Masculinity, Sport and Exercise,
https://doi.org/10.1007/978-3-030-87375-2_2

Plate wealthy—Boca Juniors working class), and disability. Yet no one ever thinks about it as a way of social segregation?

On the other hand, LGBT sport clubs are usually much more inclusive and respectful of diversity than any other mainstream clubs, due to the pure cultural, religious, socio-economic diversity of the LGBT community. It is for this reason that it is not strange to find straight people playing alongside queer people in LGBT sport clubs.

We now turn our attention as to why people desire to play in LGBT clubs. We begin by examining gay males. For them, the greatest motivation to be part of a sports club with athletes of the same sexual orientation is rooted in seeking a place where they can behave without having to hide their sexual orientation. Other reasons may include, expanding their social circle, being an active party in the community, doing social activism, or seeking romantic partners; everyone might have a different reason (Jarvis, 2015).

While we often think of these clubs as promoting political activism, individuals joining LGBT clubs do not have this activism as their main reason to join. Furthermore, the implicit political activism that show these clubs is often a barrier to those that are still assuming their own homosexuality, as they reject being part of the LGBT community, that is, until they have managed to fight their own internalized homophobia (Williamson, 2000).

In the case of lesbian females, the *machismo* that we can find in the sports world causes a general discrimination against women's sport, which is why mainstream women's sporting clubs are more open to all kinds of diversity including sexual orientation. For lesbians, the motivation to join a LGBT sport club tends to come in a higher percentage for the social part, to meet people with whom they share more than a passion for sports, than to carry out certain social activism.

Given the importance of football in Spain and Latin American societies, the discussion in this chapter will focus on the situation related to homosexuality (basically male) and football, although most of the statements could be also applied to most sports, especially in team sports.

As we mentioned earlier, a fairly common criticism of LGBT sport clubs is that this kind of clubs segregate rather than integrate LGBT people into mainstream clubs so they could become more accepting on homosexuality. This is a theoretically valid starting point. It is what should be in an ideal world where we are all equal. Unfortunately, this is not what happens in the real world, where LGBT people have to face prejudice and discrimination. In addition, LGBT people can get many benefits on a psychosocial level just for participating in this type of clubs and in LGBT competitions (Krane et al., 2002). In short, the homophobia which they face doesn't come only from other participants, but they even have to face their own internalized homophobia, because of the negative messages that they receive in mainstream clubs. Some authors, however, think that it is not clear if the development of LGBT clubs should be interpreted as a sign of political empowerment or as a sign of exclusion or even subtle discrimination by mainstream sport clubs (Elling et al., 2003; Wellard, 2002).

In Spain and Latin American countries, there are rarely examples of athletes who have "dared" to come out of the closet. Society is so permeated by *machismo* and homophobia (Aguayo & Nascimento, 2016) and especially in sports, that they make it practically impossible. Only a few cases are known (Víctor Gutiérrez, Lola Gallardo, Mapi León, Kike Sarasola, Javier Raya, Mara Gómez, Sebastián Vega, Rafaela Silva, Ian Matos among others), most of them in female sports or in male non-mainstream sports. If there are no open elite athletes, LGBT kids don't have idols in sports that can act as a role model for them.

Most children start playing sports at a very young age. The practice of a team sport is socially attributed to promoting many important values in children's emotional maturation and personality development. Positive attributes that are socially ascribed to sport also include: The collective effort over the individual, the sacrifice, the perseverance, the responsibility, the solidarity, the competitiveness, the companionship, the discipline, the respect to the authority in the figure of the coach or the referee are some of the values that are considered to contribute by practicing sport in a team. Nevertheless, at an early age, the prevailing *machismo* in Latin American societies imposes on boys the practice of a so-called masculine sport with the supremacy of football (Tajer, 1998) and practically excludes girls from sports beyond gymnastics, tennis, or volleyball. The fact that football is so important in our societies means that practically the first gift kids remember is a football ball that a father, an uncle, a grandfather give them. Football is part of a kid's life almost from the beginning (Llopis-Goig, 2010; Martín & García-Manso, 2011). In addition to this, football becomes very popular because you can practice it everywhere; only a ball and anything that can act as a goal is needed. This simplicity makes it a favorite street game for many kids in Latin America and Spain.

However, it is because of this *machismo*, which is so present in the society, and in sport, that those children who may feel different or that they don't fit in that specific category generate a rejection of sports in general, and football in particular. The values that are supposed to have when playing football such as strength, violence, or extreme competitiveness (Martín & García-Manso, 2011; Sandersson et al., 2016) are obstacles to the integration of diversity. This often leads to discrimination against these children, since by not participating in the major boy's social activity, they are forced to participate in social activities with the girls and to be discriminated against by their own mates with all kinds of insults such as sissy, girlie (*mariquita, nenaza*).

In the case of girls, those who opt into "masculine" sports are also the object of mockery and they are called butch (*marimacho*) (Jakubowska & Byczkowska-Owczarek, 2018; Martín-Horcajo, 2006). In short *machismo* keeps many LGTBIQ boys and girls away from practicing sports at an early age.

Also, in school, football is an element of socialization with the rest of the male children, both during playtime and during sports activity. Often, the leader in the class is not the one with the best grades, but the one who plays better football. Thus, those people who are closer to the corporal pattern improve their position compared to others, increasing what Bourdieu (2002) calls social capital (Piedra, 2016).

As we have seen the consequence of *machismo* in sport is the rejection of many LGBT people to the practice of sports, and those who practice sports do it in an environment that is eminently hostile to everything that separates them from the norm (Davis-Delano, 2014; Griffin, 1998; Krane, 1997; O'Brien et al., 2013; Pronger, 2000).

LGBT SPORTS CLUBS AND LGBT GENERALIST ASSOCIATIONS

As explained in the previous section, belonging to a LGBT sports club implies a certain degree of social activism by every individual who joins the club. The visibility of LGBT people practicing sport both amateur and at a professional level is necessary in order to put the issue of homophobia in sports on the political agenda, as it has a widespread presence and sometimes even unconsciously, in the sports world. On the other hand, belonging to most LGBT generalist associations requires the intention of the individual to carry out an activism to fight against a situation of inequality and discrimination of a collective.

Until the beginning of this century, LGBT sports clubs were not very welcomed by many generalist LGBT associations, as sport clubs fought for equality mainly through visibility practicing sports and not through activism. Even though most of the first LGBT sports clubs in Latin America had some kind of connection with generalist associations in their beginnings, they were never really part of them. As soon as legal equality for LGBT people (marriage and adoption in most cases) was conquered in certain countries, the generalist LGBT associations went into crisis and were reluctant to transform their goals in order to adapt to the new legal situation. This gave an opportunity to non-generalist, specific associations, among which were the LGBT sport clubs to gain acceptance and popularity, becoming even the object of attention by the generalist activism. In fact, it's clear that the contribution which LGBT sport clubs made to the cause of LGBT rights was the approach to a passive activism of many people who had not felt or willing to be represented by the generalist activism, helping in this way the so-called social normalization of LGBT rights.

The first LGBT sports clubs in Spain emerged in the mid-1990s in Barcelona and Madrid. The first steps of the Panteres Grogues club in Barcelona date back to 1994, with the practice of beach volleyball, followed shortly after by the Club Deportivo Alternativo de Madrid in 1995. In Latin America, the first club, Real Centro, started in 1990 in Brazil, but had no international presence; while in 1997, the Buenos Aires DAG (Gay Argentine Sportsmen) was formed and their football team managed to participate in the Gay Games of Amsterdam the year after, being the first presence of a full group of Latin America in any main international LGBT competition. That's a remarkable milestone for Latin LGBT clubs as until then, there had only been participants of Latin American countries integrated in European clubs or in individual sports such as swimming, tennis, and squash.

With the beginning of the twenty-first century there was an explosion of LGBT sports clubs throughout Spain and Portugal, as well as in different countries in Latin America such as Mexico, Uruguay, and Chile. The visibility and support that these first LGBT sports clubs gave to the newly created clubs no longer required to stablish collaboration with LGBT generalist collectives. Besides this, the media started to look at these clubs as something new, although kind of weird, so they got a lot of exposure in both general and sports media that also helped the growth of the existing clubs or the creation of new ones.

The existence of national and international umbrella organizations of the different LGBT clubs has benefited the creation and consolidation of clubs in different parts of the world. Among the most important, we can mention the Federation of Gay Games, GLISA (Gay and Lesbian International Sports Association), EGLSF (European Gay and Lesbian Sports Federation) or at the level of Spain, the ADI (Iberian LGBT Sports Association).

The network facilitated by those umbrella organizations to individuals trying to start new clubs was the trigger of several clubs in mid-sized cities, as well as a support for joint participation in international competitions to the newer clubs. While in the USA and Europe, these umbrella organizations were formed by different clubs, in Latin America, the cooperation took a different pattern. The clubs themselves were networking with people in other areas or countries where branches of the club were created having the same name and the territory that they cover. The most important examples are GAPEF (Gays Passionate About Football), originally from Argentina, but now with branches in Colombia, México and Chile, or Lobos who started in Mexico City and they are now present in Puebla (Mexico), Peru, Argentina, or even in the USA, where Latinos count for an important part of the society.

LGBT SPORTS CLUBS RELATIONS WITH MAINSTREAM SPORTS

It has not been easy for LGBT sports clubs to cooperate with mainstream sports, either at the club level or among sports federations. It all started when Tom Waddell (American athlete who competed at the 1968 Olympic Games in Mexico in Decathlon) and others thought that the best way to make visible the presence of homosexual athletes in sport was by creating a big amateur sports competition aimed at gay and lesbian athletes and created in 1982 the Gay Olympic Games in San Francisco. He was sued by the USOC (United States Olympic Committee) and the International Olympic Committee (IOC) for the use of the word Olympic, three weeks before its start. The organizers of the Gay Olympic Games argued that if there were other organizations that used the word Olympic, such as the Police Olympics, they could also use it, so the lawsuit was clearly discriminatory. Yet they lost the lawsuit.

After losing the lawsuit, the organizers had to remove the word Olympics and was later called Gay Games, which is still used today. Since then, many things have changed and the two organizations (Federation of the Gay Games and IOC) have established collaboration mechanisms on issues related to homophobia in sport and HIV issues.

The most important LGBT sporting event that has ever been held in Spanish and Latin American context was the EuroGames 2008 in Barcelona. This was a sports competition aimed at the LGBT European athletes. The motto of the event was "Come South, Play with us!" as the 11 previous editions were all held in Northern Europe. In occasion to the Barcelona EuroGames, organized by the local LGBT sports club, Panteres Grogues, this club contacted both the Spanish Higher Sports Council (CSD) as well as the Catalan Sports Federations Committee (UFEC) to obtain their support and involvement. The institutional support of both organizations as well as the institutional support of most of the Catalan sports federations was obtained.

It was a small step in tackling homophobia in Spanish sport, but no specific actions have been taken in the fight against homophobia in this part of the world since. The Mexican city of Guadalajara was one of the three candidates that got to the final round to celebrate the 2022 Gay Games, but was not elected. If Guadalajara had been selected, it would have been a momentous moment for making LGBT amateur sport visible in all Latin American countries. There's still hope, however for Spanish and Latin-American countries: at the time of writing this chapter, Guadalajara has been nominated again finalist to hold the 2026 Gay Games together with the Spanish city of Valencia.

The visibility of the gay community in amateur sports has been received with a diversity of opinions from players of mainstream teams on the pitch (Willis, 2015). It has been pretty common that gay players had to listen to homophobic comments coming from players of the opposing teams or even from their supporters, especially in football. Football is the last place where "true masculinity" may be lived and expressed both on and off the field (Walther, 2006) and therefore gay football players have threatened the last space where masculinity norms (although obviously obsolete for the world in which we live in) remain in force and men act as men. This happens at least at an amateur level, as there are very few, if any, cases of active elite footballers who have come out of the closet. It is in fact the lack of these publicly elite footballers what makes difficult the complete normalization and effectively tackling discrimination (Willis, 2015).

At a professional level, occasions in which an athlete comes out of the closet are rare, as there are only a few cases known, but is also not common for them to publicly express opinions about homosexuality and /or about the existence of gay in the sports world even after they retired. In most cases, in Latin American societies, the subject of sexual orientation is only brought up to make denigrating comments on an athlete or to remain as rumors with the intention that the athlete in question has the stigma of potentially being gay. For example, in 2007, the Spanish gay magazine Zero contacted a group of professional football players from several teams of *La Liga* so they would come out of the closet on a special report in the magazine, but they turned back the offer last-minute, probably because of the fear of being harassed by the environment, especially the fans and pressure from the presidents and the board of directors of the clubs.

The difference in the treatment of this issue in Anglo-Saxon societies and Latin societies is huge (see chapter of Piedra et al. in this book). In Anglo-Saxon societies there is a growing presence of gay and lesbian athletes due to the involvement of Federations and sports clubs and their campaigns to make visible and tackle homophobia, starting to recognize the existence of obstacles for gay and lesbians athletes to openly talk about their sexual orientation, and therefore establishing mechanisms to fight homophobia. In this sense, the works of sports sociologist, Eric Anderson, point out the declining in these societies of what he called homohysteria (Anderson, 2009; Anderson et al., 2016). In these societies, although homophobia continues to exist, there is not as much fear of talking about sexual orientation, nor of transgressing the stereotypes assigned to men and women.

In the case of Spain, the recent work of Piedra et al. (2017), demonstrates the cultural differences between Anglo-Saxon and Hispanic cultures, where there is a more frequent positioning to remain politically correct (see next chapter of Piedra et al. in this book). There are no scientific studies in Latin American sports showing the real situation, but sports federations keep denying that there is homosexuality in sport, thus avoiding recognition that there is discrimination.

Even in those countries where equal rights have been granted for LGBT people (such as Spain, Uruguay, Argentina, or Mexico), at a sporting level, homosexuality continues to remain taboo. As an example, at the Olympic Games in London in 2012 there were 23 openly LGBT athletes, of which there was only one Brazilian athlete. At the Rio

Olympic Games in 2016, 56 athletes were out,[1] of which only 6 athletes (5 women and 1 Brazilian man) came from Latin American countries. The high presence of Brazilian athletes in the list is determined by the increase of athletes from Brazil to be the host country. At the Tokio Games in 2021, a record number of 185 was reached,[2] of which 18 came from Brazil, 3 from Chile, 2 from Puerto Rico, 2 from Argentina, 2 from Mexico, 1 from Venezuela, 1 from Trinidad, and 1 from Peru.

Lastly, special mention has to be made in this chapter to observe the situation of transgender and intersex athletes, especially for female athletes. Since sports are segmented by assigned sex, those athletes whose assigned sex does not correspond to their gender identity or those who have a hormonal load similar to that of the other sex have to face an extra layer of difficulty in practicing sport, either at the amateur or professional level. The regulation by the International Olympic Committee of not requiring gender test per se in female registered athletes for the Olympic Games in Rio in 2016, enabled de facto the participation of intersex and transgender at the highest competitive level. In Tokio 2021, the first trans athlete compited in weighlifting.

In the case of trans athletes, the controversy usually comes when they want to participate in female competitions, because of the physical superiority of males in most sports, but also male trans have to overcome a long journey to join competitions in their preferred gender category because of the lack of regulation. Therefore, it is necessary to establish, at a national and international level, a regulation to determine the suitability of an athlete to compete according to the athlete's gender identity or the sex assigned, and not at a federation level on a case-by-case basis.

In Spain, some federations (volleyball, futsal and American football) have allowed the participation of transgender athletes in official competitions as the gender identified by the athlete. During the discussion of the law for the real and effective equality of trans people in Spain, the president of the Spanish Olympic Committee made an unfortunate comment saying that allowing trans women to participate in female competitions would only harm "real" female athletes.

In Latin America, there was a single attempt to regulate the presence of trans athletes through the National Sports Plan of Peru in May 2017, in compliance with the principle of non-discrimination, but the part related to gender identity was repealed after strong lobbying efforts on the part of conservative groups. Although the status of trans people was not specifically regulated in the national sporting bodies, the Colombian trans athlete, Yanelle Zape, was very close to qualify for the Rio Olympics in 2016. Equally important to mention the case of the trans Argentinian football player, Mara Gomez, who was the first trans woman to participate in the national female league in 2020.

How Does Legal Protection Situation of LGBT Rights in Latin American Countries Affect the Creation and Growth of LGBT Clubs?

The societies of Latin American countries have some points in common that influence the way in which legal and social equality of gays, lesbian, and trans people are perceived, despite the economic, political, social, and cultural differences that may be found in each of these countries. The common denominator, whose incidence is more significant, is the power and the influence that the Catholic Church had (and still has in some countries) in the different Latin American communities. The belligerence with which the Catholic Church has approached homosexuality and transgender issues is well known (Aguiló, 2010; Mott, 2010), so in more Catholic societies, LGBT people have greater difficulty in expressing their sexual orientation (Leal, 2017), even within close circles of friends and family.

This difficulty, and the lack of positive references not only at a sporting level, but also at a political, cultural level, facilitates LGBT people into joining clubs and associations in which they can express themselves with greater freedom. LGBT sports clubs play an essential role in achieving that goal, being spaces in which besides practicing sport, they have the opportunity to meet other people who are in the same situation, and support each other in the process of coming out of the closet with the family, school, or workmates; as well as making friends outside the traditional circuits of nightlife or dating apps.

The legal framework protecting the rights of LGBT people, or at least their inclusion in the political agenda, plays an important role in the development of LGBT sport clubs. Once legal equality has been achieved, LGBT people can aim to achieve social equality, including in their leisure activities. Currently, equal marriage is legislated regulated in Spain, Argentina, Uruguay, Brazil, Colombia, Ecuador, and some states in Mexico. In Chile and Peru, a draft about Equal Marriage Law is being prepared, which is expected to be approved in the coming years.

The attached table shows the list of the LGBT clubs founded in every country and the date in which equal marriage laws were passed. A relationship between the creation of sports clubs in these countries and advances at the legislative level with the approval of equal marriage and other protection of LGBT rights can then be established (Table 2.1).

You can see the relationship between establishing legal equality (first) and then the promotion of social equality for LGBT people above. LGBT sports clubs play a very important role in social equality by making

Table 2.1 List of LGBT Latin American and Spanish clubs and date of creation

Club	City	Country	Creation	Equality laws in the country
Real Centro SP	São Paulo	Brazil	1990	2013
Panteres Grogues	Barcelona	Spain	1994	2005
CD Alternativo	Madrid	Spain	1997	2005
MadPoint	Madrid	Spain	1997	2005
Dogos (DAG)	Buenos Aires	Argentina	1997	2010
Halegatos	Madrid	Spain	1999	2005
Elaios	Zaragoza	Spain	2003	2010
Samarucs	Valencia	Spain	2003	2005
Hegosport	Bilbao	Spain	2004	2005
Lobos	Mexico DF	Mexico	2004	2010 (DF)
Halcones	Mexico DF	Mexico	2004	2010 (DF)
Condores Chile	Santiago	Chile	2006	
Uruguay Celeste	Montevideo	Uruguay	2006	2013
SAFG	Buenos Aires	Argentina	2007	2010
BJWHF	Lisbon	Portugal	2009	2010
GMadrid	Madrid	Spain	2010	2010
Didesex	Mexico DF	Mexico	2010	2010 (DF)
Spartans	Porto	Portugal	2010	2010
GAPEF	Buenos Aires	Argentina	2010	2010
Titanes	Madrid	Spain	2013	2010
GAPEF	Bogotá	Colombia	2015	2016
GAPEF	Mexico DF	Mexico	2016	2010 (DF)
GAPEF	Santiago	Chile	2016	
Lobos	Buenos Aires	Argentina	2016	2010
BeesCats	Rio de Janeiro	Brazil	2017	2013
Lobos	Lima	Peru	2017	
Diversport	Torremolinos	Spain	2018	2005

LGBT athletes visible in the sports world. In the same sense, due to the growing social acceptance of sexual diversity, many more LGBT people are attracted to sports in sport clubs or informal LGBT groups (Elling et al., 2003). On the other hand, in those countries where LGBT rights have not been permitted, it is much more difficult to create safe sports spaces, as the LGBT issues still have to be introduced in the political agenda, as well as in different layers of a society strongly influenced by the Catholic Church, *machismo* and tradition. In this situation we would find countries like Bolivia, or Paraguay, where LGBT activism is still in a fairly emergent position.

THE FUTURE OF LGBT SPORTS CLUBS

In an ideal world, where no one had to face any type of direct or indirect discrimination when it comes to practicing their favorite sport at an amateur level, LGBT sports clubs should not have a reason to exist. They would lack one of its main purposes, such as offering a space free of discrimination where everyone can be themselves without the fear that this would affect their relationship with the rest of the members of the club or their leaders. Therefore, the goal of any LGBT sports club should be to disappear once the objectives have been met, or to become a social sports club without any political content or claim.

Unfortunately, this situation is still very far from us. Very few elite athletes in Latin American societies can be a role model for the thousands of LGBT children, teenagers, and adults who may need their support in the difficult process of self-acceptance and coming to terms regarding their sexuality with their friends and relatives. The only presence of LGBT people in sports is to be found in this kind of clubs. There are obviously LGBT athletes in elite sports, just by means of percentage in the society in general. Why there is not a single athlete in any professional league of any sport in any Latin American country who has openly expressed to be LGBT? If the percentage of LGBT people in relation to the general population is between 5 and 10%, why are there so few professional elite athletes among them? One of the characteristics of homophobia in sport is precisely its subtlety. Almost none is directly discriminated against for being gay but the hostility of the environment acts as a deterrent and produces a need to make sexual orientation invisible or give up sports.

It is our argument that we all need to work together to promote an environment so that any LGBT athlete can come out of the closet without risking their sporting career, their sponsors, their relationship with the media, and their supporters in the stands. Our society needs a sport world that recognizes diversity, that enables everyone to express themselves as they really are and not as they are supposed to be.

NOTE

1. https://www.outsports.com/2016/7/11/12133594/rio-oly mpics-teams-2016-gay-lgbt-athletes-record.
2. https://www.outsports.com/olympics/2021/7/12/22565574/ tokyo-summer-olympics-lgbtq-gay-athletes-list.

REFERENCES

Aguayo, F., & Nascimento, M. (2016). Dos décadas de estudios de hombres y masculinidades en América Latina: Avances y desafíos [Two decades of studies of men and masculinities in Latin America: Advances and challenges]. *Sexualidad, Salud y Sociedad - Revista Latinoamericana, 22*, 207–220. https://doi.org/10.1590/1984-6487.sess.2016.22.09.a

Aguiló, A. J. (2010). Pensamiento abismal, diferenciación sexual desigual y homofobia eclesial' [Abysmal thinking, uneven sexual differentiation and ecclesiastic homophobia]. *Nómada. Revista Crítica de Ciencias Sociales y Jurídicas, 23*(3), 1–22.

Anderson, E. (2009). *Inclusive masculinity: The changing nature of masculinities.* Routledge.

Anderson, E., Magrath, R., & Bullingham, R. (2016). *Out in sport. The experiences of openly gay and lesbian athletes in competitive sport.* Routledge.

Bourdieu, P. (2002). *Masculine domination.* Stanford University Press.

Davis-Delano, L. R. (2014). Sport as context for the development of women's same-sex relationships. *Journal of Sport & Social Issues, 38*(3), 263–285. https://doi.org/10.1177/0193723513520554

Elling, A., De Knop, P., & Knoppers, A. (2003). Gay/lesbian sport clubs and events. Places of homo-social bonding and cultural resistance? *International Review for the Sociology of Sport, 38*(4), 441–456. https://doi.org/10.1177/1012690203384005

Griffin, P. (1998). *Strong women, deep closet: Lesbian and homophobia in sport.* Human Kinetics.

Jakubowska, H., & Byczkowska-Owczarek, D. (2018). Girls in football, boys in dance. Stereotypization processes in socialization of young sportsmen and sportswomen. *Qualitative Sociology Review*, *14*(2), 12–28. https://doi.org/10.18778/1733-8077.14.2.02

Jarvis, N. (2015). The inclusive masculinities of heterosexual men within UK gay sport clubs. *International Review for the Sociology of Sport*, *50*(3), 283–300. https://doi.org/10.1177/1012690213482481

Krane, V. (1997). Homonegativism experienced by lesbian collegiate athletes. *Women in Sport & Physical Activity Journal*, *6*(1), 141–163. https://doi.org/10.1123/wspaj.6.2.141

Krane, V., Barber, H., & McClung, L. (2002). Social psychological benefits of Gay Games participation: A Social Identity Theory explanation. *Journal of Applied Sport Psychology*, *14*(1), 27–42. https://doi.org/10.1080/10413200209339009

Leal, L. E. (2017). Identidad sexual y pertenencia eclesial. Derroteros de visibilidad en trayectorias de gays católicos [Sexual identity and church belonging. Visibility paths in the careers of gay Catholics]. *Sexualidad Salud y Sociedad. Revista Latinoamericana*, *26*, 262–278. https://doi.org/10.1590/1984-6487.sess.2017.26.13.a

Llopis-Goig, R. (2010). Masculinidades Inductoras. La construcción de la masculinidad en el fútbol español [Inductor Masculinities. The Construction Of Masculinity In Spanish Football]. *Sistema. Revista De Ciencias Sociales*, *217*, 61–76.

Martín, A., & García-Manso, A. (2011). Construyendo la masculinidad: Fútbol, violencia e identidad [Doing masculinity: Football, violence and identity]. *Revista De Investigaciones Políticas y Sociológicas*, *10*(2), 73–95.

Martín-Horcajo, M. (2006). Contribución del feminismo de la diferencia sexual a los análisis de género en el deporte [The contribution of sexual difference feminism to the analysis of gender within sport]. *Revista Internacional De Sociología*, *44*, 111–131. https://doi.org/10.3989/ris.2006.i44.30

Mott, L. (2010). Del malo pecado al pecado intrínsecamente malo: La radicalización fundamentalista de la homofobia católica desde los tiempos de la Inquisición hasta Benedicto XVI. *Historia*, *29*(1), 4–23. https://doi.org/10.1590/S0101-90742010000100002

O'Brien, K. S., Shovelton, H., & Latner, J. D. (2013). Homophobia in physical education and sport: The role of physical/sporting identity and attributes, authoritarian aggression, and social dominance orientation [From a grave sin to a sin that is intrinsically grave: The fundamentalist radicalization of catholic homophobia from the era of the Inquisition to Benedict XVI]. *International Journal of Psychology*, *48*(5), 891–899. https://doi.org/10.1590/S0101-90742010000100002

Piedra, J. (2016). *Deporte y Género. Manual de Iniciación* [Gender and Sport. Handbook for beginning]. INDE.

Piedra, J., García-Pérez, R., & Channon, A. (2017). Between Homohysteria and Inclusivity: Tolerance towards sexual diversity in sport. *Sexuality and Culture, 21*(4), 1018–1039. https://doi.org/10.1007/s12119-017-9434-x

Pronger, B. (2000). Homosexuality and sport. Who's winning? In J. McKay, M.A. Messner, & D. Sabo (Eds.), *Masculinities, gender relations, and sport* (pp. 222–244). SAGE.

Sandersson, J., Weathers, M., Grevious, A., Tehan, M., & Warren, S. (2016). A hero or sissy? Exploring media framing of NFL quarterbacks injury decisions. *Communication & Sport, 4*(1), 3–22. https://doi.org/10.1177/216747951 4536982

Tajer, D. (1998). El fútbol como organizador de la masculinidad. *La Ventana, 8*, 248–268.

Walther , T. (2006). *Kick it out. Homophobia in football.* European Gay and Lesbian Sport Federation.

Wellard, I. (2002). Men, sport, body performance and the maintenance of 'exclusive masculinity. *Leisure Studies, 21*, 235–247. https://doi.org/10.1080/026 1436022000030641

Williamson, I. (2000). Internalized homophobia and health issues affecting lesbian and gay men. *Health Education Research, 15*(1), 97–107. https://doi.org/10.1093/her/15.1.97

Willis, T. (2015). Kicking down barriers: Gay footballers, challenging stereotypes and changing attitudes in amateur league play. *Soccer & Society, 16*(2–3), 377–392. https://doi.org/10.1080/14660970.2014.961717

CHAPTER 3

Coming Out of the Closet: A Description of LGBT Research on Sports in Brazil

Vinnicius Laurindo and Mariana Zuaneti Martins

INTRODUCTION

One who is said to come out of the closet, to have left one's *safe haven*, finds in that liberation an ocean of possibilities. Through one's becoming other, a field of difference and of areas of intersection and encounter, coming out enables a transformation of the subject as one relates to a myriad of possibilities and forces. There is a multiplication of the self in this happening of becoming. The confines of the closet fade into the distance. From the horizon emerges a place to be enjoyed (Deleuze & Guattari, 2012). The Brazilian field of research on LGBT identities in sports was, for a long time, "in the closet," cloaked in invisibility and confined to a space of taboo. Yet, in recent decades, this research area has emerged with a promising future—a becoming.

It is not just in sports that, historically, discussions about sexuality have been silenced. This secret story remains locked in the "closet of sexuality" for all (Sedgwick, 2007). The term becoming, in the sense that

V. Laurindo · M. Z. Martins (✉)
University of Espírito Santo, Vitória, Brazil

© The Author(s), under exclusive license to Springer Nature Switzerland AG 2021
J. Piedra and E. Anderson (eds.), *Lesbian, Gay, and Transgender Athletes in Latin America*, Palgrave Studies in Masculinity, Sport and Exercise, https://doi.org/10.1007/978-3-030-87375-2_3

41

Gilles Deleuze and Félix Guattari use it, attends to the process of resistance to and separation from the closet, questioning the norms that are linked to certain genders and sexualities. "Coming out" of the closet can therefore be a kind of "rite" of passage, by means of an affirmation of a non-heterosexual orientation (Camargo, 2016). Thus, it is possible to identify a tension with and points of departure from the established order.

Sexuality is a device that is constituted from the discourses that regulate, normalize, and produce truths about sex (Foucault, 2019). Although the heterosexual matrix is constituted by the alignment of sex-gender-desire, in the scientific field in recent decades, the presence of non-normalized sexualities and the diverse gender identities that are outside the male/female, homosexual/heterosexual binary circuits (Louro, 2008) are "coming out of the closet." This visibility comes in the wake of a civil organization of a political nature known as LGBT (Lesbian, Gay, Bisexual, and Transsexual), which in Brazil started gaining momentum in the 1970s with identity politics (Facchini & França, 2009).

Although the expansion of public spaces related to homosexuality has been registered since the 1970s, research in Brazil on this field emerged in the 1980s, mainly portraying spaces of homosexual sociability (Simões & Facchini, 2009). However, it was only at the end of the first decade of the 2000s that this "coming out of the closet" also had an impact on Brazilian descriptions of sports, pointing to a very recent field of research that therefore contains a series of gaps and a substantial research agenda, yet to be developed.

Brazilian studies on sport and gender are increasing. However, this growth is small when compared to the international scenario, and when it addresses the intersection of sexuality (Goellner, 2012). Thus, sports in Brazil were and still are shut in the closet of sexuality. Little by little, LGBT sports collectives have begun to emerge, such as volleyball and football (a term which here refers to what some North Americans call soccer) teams, dodgeball festivals (*festivais de queimada*), and football supporter groups. This occupation of spaces is a way of reshaping mainstream sport and, in this sense, LGBT sport may offer interesting elements to rethink the sports system (Camargo & Kessler, 2017). Considering that scenario, this chapter presents a description of how the LGBT population has been narrated in research on sports in Brazil. This description seeks to offer a "state of the art" (Ferreira, 2002) of Brazilian academic production on LGBT identities in sports, by reviewing what has been investigated in the country's graduate programs, from 2003, when the first thesis on the subject was defended, to 2019.

To this end, we conducted a survey of the production of master's theses (known in Portuguese as *dissertações*) and doctoral dissertations (in Portuguese, *teses*) published in the catalog of theses and dissertations on the Coordination for the Improvement of Higher Education Personnel (CAPES) website (www.capes.gov.br). This state of the art was conducted on the CAPES thesis and dissertations catalog in May 2020, and was carried out by two researchers, with no specific time frame. In the process of searching for theses and dissertations, we used a combination of the following descriptors "lesb* AND esport*," "homossexual* AND esport*," "homofobia AND esport*," "gay* AND esport*," "trans-gener* AND esport*," and "homofobia AND futebol" (words which mean in English: lesb* AND sports*," "homosexuality* AND sports*," "homophobia* AND sports*," "gay* AND sports*," "transsexual* AND sports*," and "homophobia* AND football*"). Some of the documents that appeared in the search did not specifically address the theme and (14 works) were therefore excluded.

The works that did address the theme totaled 18 publications: 12 master's theses and six doctoral dissertations. The first work was completed in 2003 and the second in 2008. Between 2008 and 2014, seven related works were defended; from 2015 to 2019, there were ten works defended, showing an increase in interest in the theme, especially since 2018. This shows that sexuality/sexual identity in sports has aroused greater interest among Brazilian researchers in the last decade in situations that concern affective issues and sociability, homophobia, masculinities, transphobia, and dissonant practices in sports (Camargo, 2016).

The subjects addressed also changed over time. In general, there is a great interest in football in the LGBT research. The first studies present reflections on football as a space for lesbian sociability, but lately male homosexuality has been dominating research agendas. While the research on lesbians in football focuses on sports as a space of sociability, when it comes to the description of gays in football, the focus is on homophobia, showing two different research perspectives.

In addition, almost all studies involving male homosexuality deal with fan culture, which shows that addressing the sexuality of football players is still taboo, even in academic research. In the last decade, there has been a process of describing inclusive masculinities in sports; there is a trend in the development of dissonant practices that contrasts traditional ways of doing sports with being in sports as well as research on transgender subjects in sports. Below, we offer a narrative synthesis of these trends and some problematization around the gaps, silences, and of research on LGBT people in sports, which we would characterize as being in a process of coming out of the closet, a becoming.

Football as a Space for Lesbian Sociability

The field of research on LGBT subjects in sports was inaugurated with research on the practice of women's football. Interest in this subject derives from gender studies and studies on women in sports, which have been increasingly present in the literature since the late 1990s. At the intersections of gender, in the transgressions of normalized femininity and the heterosexual matrix, women's football has also presented itself as a fruitful field for debates on sexuality. Despite the initial awakening to this theme, it has not predominated over the years. Rather, studies on male homosexuality and transgender have emerged, which did not altogether push studies of women's football and sexuality into obscurity. Research, especially on lesbians in football, remains present.

In many dissertations or thesis, women's football has been highlighted as a favorable space for the creation of networks and associations, where affect is one of the central elements (Giarola, 2003; Jardim, 2013; Pisani, 2018; Silveira, 2008). These networks tend to help women deal with the violent context in which they are inserted, as well as to welcome and value the performatization of non-normalized femininities (Pisani, 2018). Thus, for these women, playing football, in addition to leisure, involves the establishment of affective/sexual relationships, strengthening the networks of associations promoted from that space (Jardim, 2013).

Football is, at the same time, a welcoming space for transgressive performances and dissident sexual practices, as well as a place of violence in its attempts to normalize bodies and make abject some of the people who participate in this sport. In this sense, research shows how football has represented, for women practitioners, a more welcoming space for dissident sexualities. However, even so, identifying as "lesbian" (or coming out) has not been easy, as it is still considered taboo. In the meantime, sexuality intersecting with gender may suggest an even greater obstacle to the affirmation of sexuality (Silveira, 2008) bearing in mind that some players challenge the normative definitions of femininity (Scott, 1995), when they show themselves as strong and aggressive.

Mariane Pisani (2018), in her dissertation on football as a leisure activity for women, describes a paradox of this scenario in women's football. The traditional media represented black women with a more "masculinized" gender performance based on metaphors from nature. The metaphor of "beasts" (in Portuguese, *feras*), in contrast to white players and a normalized femininity, called "beautiful," discursively located these transgressive corporealities as "bestial" or animalistic, products of an uncontrollable and uncivilized nature (Pisani, 2018). By positioning them as animals, they are removed from the field of rationality and their "humanity" is denigrated, thus violating them in metaphorical abjection.

This refers to an abject body, as it is placed at the frontier limits of normative bodies, considered, therefore, to deviate from the norm. As Butler (2019) signals, there is a constructed character of the body taken as an intertwining of borders that gains political significance. The transgression of lesbian women occurs in many ways, and in some circumstances they perform through the body, through gestures and attitudes, forms of resistance that are productive, but which also put them on the sidelines.

On the other hand, in the field of everyday practices, Mariane Pisani (2018) reaffirms football as a useful space to perform transgressive femininities and dissident sexualities. It is important to say that the sexuality of these lesbian women is designed in the intersectionality of other social markers. Race, gender, class, generation, and nationality affect sexual identity, so they also interfere in the way of living this identity (Weeks, 2000). For example, women who were the subjects of ethnographies by Pisani (2018) fetishized the bodies of lesbian women whose performance was more masculine. In contrast, those who reiterated normalized femininity were discriminated against by other women, reversing the power relations and the prevalent classifications in cultural discourses.

In this way, the sociability developed by these women in football brings them closer to a sense of community (Carter & Baliko, 2017). The many women who interconnect through sports do so because of a cultural affinity. These community spaces are fundamental for the formation and maintenance of lesbian identities, as they provide a safe place to negotiate issues related to family conflicts and also represent a way to find new friends (Valentine, 2002). Furthermore, these women share an identity, a purpose, and a set of beliefs. These are, therefore, safe spaces of support.

MALE HOMOSEXUALITY
AND HOMOHYSTERIA ENTER THE FIELD

If the field of research had its emergence or "coming out" following studies of gender and women in sports, its recent development has pointed to the debate on male homosexuality in football, which corresponds to one third of the related research. Such research addresses the fan culture in football and the manifestations and discourses of homophobia.

From a historical point of view, Rodrigo Rosa (2010), in his dissertation on LGBT sports history in Brazil, analyzed the narratives carried out by homophobia in sports in gay magazines, from 1978 to 2007. In the publications, there is a predominance of statements about football, in which there is an appreciation of some masculinities and contempt for others. In this way, the football space feeds back prejudices, discrimination, and multiple forms of violence against homosexual, bisexual, and transgender people. Staying "closeted," in this sense, can mean staying safe for those men who live in the football universe. In contrast, "coming out" can elicit hateful homophobic responses.

Although a useful alternative, the closet represents the silencing and confinement of subjectivities and the different ways of being masculine in the world. Gay fans, for example, suffer from homophobia in stadiums and from the experience of chants or cheers, although some of them do not understand certain manifestations as the result of their exclusion or prejudice, as José Silva Junior describes in his dissertation on gay football fandom (Silva Júnior, 2018). According to Luiz Fernando Lemes, in his thesis about homophobia in football fandom, the media usually attributes other meanings to the insults and behaviors experienced in the stadium, as if homophobic offenses were part of that cultural atmosphere (Lemes, 2019). In general, they take ownership of these territories, produce and reproduce heterosexist and homophobic behavior in a similar way to other fans, aligned with a heteronormative logic of cheering (Silva Júnior, 2018), facing symbolic domination as a part of a survival tactic in that space.

As Gustavo Bandeira describes in his dissertation on masculinities in football fandom, such behaviors are the result of a curriculum of masculinity of those supporters in the stadium, one which produces a stratification of bodies and behaviors in the supporter culture (Bandeira, 2009, 2017). There is a strong presence of homophobic verbal violence, especially against the opposing team's fans.

On the other hand, it is possible to perceive a "macho love" rooted in misogyny and homophobia due to the affect presented to men who are in the same crowd. This affect is possible among those men who embody the "positive"—that is, the normative—representation of masculinity. It is also perceived as a presence of discourses on subaltern masculinities, discourses that challenge the masculinity of rival fans. It is based on this differentiation of the masculinity of "our fans" in relation to "their fans," that supremacy is guaranteed. This gender performance includes, in addition to masculinity, performance of heterosexuality and heterosexism (Borrillo, 2009). According to Joaquim Sobreira Filho (2018), there are still many barriers that permeate football, either with respect to the acceptance of players with other sexual identities, or in relation to the inclusion of transgender in the sport or even with regard to the behavior of diverse fans.

In addition to football, volleyball has also been a privileged modality for the expression of homophobic discourses. The case of the professional volleyball player Michael (Anjos, 2013), who is openly homosexual, exposes the presence of the symbolic gender violence of fans in an environment that is not demarcated as masculine with the same intensity as football. As Luiza Anjos (2013) described in her dissertation, discourses in the media about episodes of homophobic cursing at the player establishes a dispute: on the one hand, the defense of less aggressive behaviors of fans in sports arenas that goes beyond the rite itself and communicates with other spheres of social life (Toledo, 2002), on the other, the legitimation of the flexibility of norms of civility and violence.

In other studies, there is a persistence of prejudice against subjects who claim to be gays or who confront gender norms (men considered effeminate, for example). This prejudice comes from several places, tending to affect the athlete's development. "Effeminate" volleyball athletes verbalize a certain difficulty in advancing their sporting career (Volpe, 2018). Their participation is restricted to teams that compete in tournaments considered to be second tier, without great prospects for the future, because in this context their acceptance is greater. Silva (2016) highlights that volleyball players suffer from homophobia, but they still assert themselves in the sport. Similarly, some of them also reproduce these prejudices. In the dissertation of Leandro Brito (2018) on inclusive masculinities in the volleyball, the young adolescents participating in this ethnographic study enunciate the imposition of hegemonic masculinity as a performance in the volleyball space-times and, mainly, in school, as they are perceived as abject and precarious bodies.

Finally, it is necessary to highlight a study that focused on homophobic acts directed at women. Carla Grespan (2014) identifies that female fighters' access to their sport is permeated by many restrictions due to the standardized representation of femininity and due to heteronormativity in the Ultimate Fighting Championship (UFC). Sexist and misogynistic behavior on the part of the readers of the researched sites eroticize and disqualify the performance of the fighters, whose presence creates tensions with the representations of virility linked to the practice. There is also a strong lesbophobic and transphobic content in the fans' commentary or comments on the sport based on an insistence on representing the fighters, based on the centrality of their bodies and their sexualities, considered abject.

DISSONANT SPORT PRACTICES

Recently, dissonant sports practices, that is, those that intend to challenge the stylized repetition of movements common to sport, have gained space in descriptive research. For example, activities which highlight non-normative bodies, such as the Paralympic games. The development of these practices is a resistance to the idea of a standard or normative gesture or a certain body composition as the most appropriate for the practitioner of a particular sport. As non-normative bodies are highlighted in this kind of events, it functions as a pressure for reframing sport's mainstream.

In the analysis of dissonant practices, Carla Grespan describes in her dissertation the insertion of women in the UFC functioning as a transgression of norms (Grespan, 2014). The muscular and dissonant bodies of the fighters, as well as the affirmation of their lesbian identities, demand other discourses, other spaces, and allow the possibility of new designs, configurations, and relations of gender, bodies, and sexualities. Perhaps, as Davies and Deckert (2020) mentioned, they are forcing a re-imagination of femininity. However, this issue contrasts with the unstable and ambivalent gendered world in which the fighters live (Knijnik & de Carvalho Ferretti, 2015).

When it comes to football and the masculinity curriculum of supporters in the stadium, Gustavo Bandeira's dissertation (2017) and Maurício Pinto's thesis (2017) show some movements that challenge the cultural dynamic of intense rivalry and competition based on a homosexually themed language (Magrath, 2017). Gay fans have gained prominence and are strengthened by some movements of fans aimed against homophobia and sexism in football, through the appropriation of identity by "*torcedorxs*" or football "fanxtics" have asserted their existence and garnered visibility for their ideals on social networks. In contrast with the English case, where Magrath (2017) showed that these homosexually themed chanting was not an expression of a homophobic attitude, but a way to diminish the rival, in Brazil, these gay groups create tension or challenge the boundaries of the virile and aggressive masculinity of fan culture (Monteiro, 2003) and, in other space-times, such as social networks, they articulate and assert their resistance and existence.

In this wake, Wagner Camargo (2012), in his dissertation, describes the LGBT world competitions, interpreting a certain paradoxical and controversial aspect in the sport practiced in these competitions. At the same time that they break with the heteronormativity of sports, constituting a possibility of practice for subjects with dissident sexualities, they still reproduce certain hierarchies that place gays and lesbians in a prominent position in such competitions, to the detriment of other gender and/or sexual identities. At the same time, the sociability between LGBT people brought about by this event is pointed out as part of the structuring logic of LGBT sporting events, functioning as an important element of socialization of the participants, also tensioning the sanitized spaces of performance-oriented sports. By highlighting dissonant practices, Camargo (2012) presents the performance of trans subjects and subversive gays as "deviations." Therefore, such performativity (Butler, 2019) cannot be understood as a distortion but must be understood as productive, as it functions with the power of producing, to see with other lenses or even to feel in another way.

Alexandre Volpe's (2018) thesis on volleyball highlights many stereotypes created due to the practice of the sport by men in Brazil, leading many practitioners to be labeled as gay. However, even though they suffer some type of violence, especially when it comes to professional sports, many players use this stigma as a power of affirmation and assert themselves as gay, resisting the demand for hegemonic masculinity in clubs (Connell, 1995). The author also highlights a strong sense of community (Carter & Baliko, 2017) among players, one that welcomes those who may have come out of the closet. The importance of commonality linked to support and mutual understanding is evident here.

In the dissertation of Leandro Brito (2018), young players pronounce subversive utterances and gender parodies, approaching a more inclusive masculinity (Anderson & McCormack, 2018). They were recognized in training spaces-times by the names of women professional volleyball players. By "confronting" opponents in volleyball competitions, by "assembling" to train and play, seeking to stage performances, these players destabilized and re-signified masculinity in their sport.

Another dissident corporeality that caused controversy in the Brazilian sports field was the presence of transgender volleyball player Tifanny on a professional team (Iwamoto, 2019). Tiago Iwamoto's dissertation on media discourses on the presence of Tifanny in the women's league showed that the participation of trans players in conventional sports raises the debate over the construction of genders, putting into question the way the sports world is structured and organized, making fissures appear and proposing, in light of these fissures, new models of organization of sports practice, possibly merging skills and technology (Iwamoto, 2019).

For a long time, transgender bodies were outside the official global sports system; however, in the early 2000s the international Olympic committee was favorable to the participation of transgender athletes in Olympic sports, subject to certain rules. The first favorable signal came in 2003 when the medical committee of the International Olympic Committee (IOC) decided in favor of the participation of trans athletes in competitions. Thirteen years later, the IOC published a new consensus with different rules (International Olympic Committee, 2015).

This theme has gained relevance in Brazil at the same time that some legislature has appeared on a regional and national scale that try to prohibit the participation of transgender/transsexual people in official sports competitions. The justifications are anchored in the alignment between the sex-gender categories—that is, cisgender men can only play in the men's category and cisgender women can only participate in the women's category due to the supposed biological differences between their bodies (Brasil, 2019a, 2019b). These bodies are not the healthy bodies (skilled and legitimate) that validate the official competitive sporting process. In general, the sports field is organized based on the male/female binary system and, therefore, disregards dissenting corporealities, relocating them in other spaces with lower status.

It is important to highlight that the social markers of difference can influence multiple masculinities. This is evident in Leandro Brito's dissertation on gay volleyball players. One participant of the research, Boskolipe said, while among children and infants, he was a regular player, when he reached the youth leagues, he became a reserve. One of the reasons that justify the change, in his view, is that he is gay, handicapped, poor, and effeminate (Brito, 2018). Evidently, this intersectionality, explored by Brito (2018) and Pisani (2018), is still an emerging trend and exposes one of the critical silences of Brazilian LGBT production. Talking about sexuality, including the intersection of class, race, generation, territory, and religion, among others, is to demarcate the place of epistemological decoloniality, fundamental to the descriptions that emerge in Latin America.

FINAL WORDS: VISIBILITIES, TABOOS, AND CRITICAL SILENCES

Brazilian research on the LGBT theme in sports is linked to some spaces of greater visibility: such as lesbian sociability in football and gay sociability in volleyball. In addition to these presences, descriptions of collectives of gay male football supporters also emerged, demonstrating a predominance of descriptions related to this sport, the most popular in the country. In this modality, the theme of sociability was portrayed in the investigations of women in football and homophobia was present in studies of men, demonstrating two different directions of research on sexualities in football, intersecting at the gender marker.

Dealing with the sexualities of football players is still taboo, and this is an important gap to be addressed, which could contribute to the reduction of prejudice. There are still few records of historical narratives of the participation of the LGBT collectives in sports, the absence of which makes it difficult to contrast them with a history of invisibility and exclusion. Still, it is worth highlighting the silencing of the intersectionality of class and race in research on the LGBT theme in Brazilian sports, something that still maintains a certain coloniality on the field.

Finally, there are two aspects that are possibly gaining space. Firstly, the description of spaces that welcome the LGBT collective, forming more inclusive masculinities and dissonant sports practices. Secondly, there is also research on transgenderism in sports, explored in the case of volleyball with the player Tifanny, whose gender identity has had a lot of repercussions in the country in recent years (Garcia & Pereira, 2020). These studies can contribute to the tensioning of norms based on the binary biological construction that has culturally organized the modern sports institutions. Such paths can bring about not only records of the sports practices of the LGBT collective, but can also contribute to challenging and rethinking mainstream sports practices.

REFERENCES

Anderson, E., & McCormack, M. (2018). Inclusive masculinity theory: Overview, reflection, and refinement. *Journal of Gender Studies, 27*(5), 547–561. https://doi.org/10.1080/09589236.2016.1245605

Anjos, L. A. D. (2013). *Quando o silêncio é rompido: homossexualidades e esportes na internet*. M.A. thesis (Leisure Studies). Universidade Federal de Minas Gerais.

Bandeira, G. A. (2009). *'Eu canto bebo e brigo...alegria do meu coração': currículo de masculinidades nos estádios de futebol*. M.A. thesis (Education). Universidade Federal do Rio Grande do Sul.

Bandeira, G. A. (2017). *Do olímpico à arena: elitização, racismo e heterossexismo no currículo de masculinidade dos torcedores de estádio*. Ph.D. dissertation (Education). Universidade Federal do Rio Grande do Sul.

Borrillo, D. (2009). A homofobia. In T. Lionço, & D. Diniz (Eds.), *Homofobia & educação: um desafio ao silêncio* (pp. 15–46). Editora UnB.

Brasil. (2019a). *Câmara dos Deputados* [Online]. https://www.camara.leg.br/proposicoesWeb/fichadetramitacao?idProposicao=2197492. Accessed 1 Oct 2020.

Brasil (2019b). *Câmara dos Deputados* [Online]. https://www.camara.leg.br/proposicoesWeb/fichadetramitacao?idProposicao=2199734&ord=1. Accessed 1 Oct 2020.

de Brito, L. T. (2018). *Enunciações de masculinidade em narrativas de jovens atletas de voleibol: leituras em horizonte queer*. Ph.D. dissertation (Education). Universidade do Estado do Rio de Janeiro.

Butler, J. (2019). *Problemas de gênero: feminismo e subversão da identidade*. Civilização Brasileira.

Camargo, W. X. (2012). *Circulando entre práticas esportivas e sexuais: etnografia em competições esportivas mundiais*. Ph.D. dissertation (Human Sciences). Universidade Federal de Santa Catarina.

Camargo, W. X. (2016). Dilemas insurgentes no esporte: as práticas esportivas dissonantes. *Movimento, 22*(4), 1337–1350. https://doi.org/10.22456/1982-8918.66188

Camargo, W. X., & Kessler, C. (2017). Além do Masculino/Feminino: Gênero, Sexualidade, Tecnologia e Performance no Esporte sob perspectiva crítica. *Horizontes Antropológicos, Porto Alegre, 23*(47), 191–225. https://doi.org/10.1590/S0104-71832017000100007

Carter, C., & Baliko, K. (2017). 'These are not my people': Queer sport spaces and the complexities of community. *Leisure Studies, 36*(5), 696–707. https://doi.org/10.1080/02614367.2017.1315164

Connell, R. (1995). *Masculinities*. University of California Press.

Davies, S. G., & Deckert, A. (2020). Muay Thai: Women, fighting, femininity. *International Review for the Sociology of Sport, 55*(3), 327–343. https://doi.org/10.1177/1012690218801300

Deleuze, G., & Guattari, F. (2012). *Mil platôs: capitalismo e esquizofrenia* (Vol. 4). Editora 34.

Facchini, R., & França, I. L. (2009). De cores e matizes: Sujeitos, conexões e desafios no Movimento LGBT brasileiro. *Sexualidad, Salud y Sociedad - Revista Latinoamericana, 3*, 54–81.

Ferreira, N. S. de A. (2002). As pesquisas denominadas 'estado da arte'. *Educação & sociedade, 23*(79), 257–272. https://doi.org/10.1590/S0101-73302002000300013

Foucault, M. (2019). *História da sexualidade I: a vontade de saber*. Paz e Terra.

Garcia, R. M., & Pereira, E. G. B. (2020). Transexualidade e esporte: o caso brasileiro de Tifanny abreu. *Educación Física y Deporte, 39*(2). https://doi.org/10.1177/1012690218801300

Giarola, W. A. (2003). Corpo mulher no esporte: a questão da prática do futebol. M.A. thesis (Physical Education). UNIMEP – Universidade Metodista de Piracicaba.

Goellner, S. V. (2012). Gender and sports in the Brazilian historiography: Overview and potentials. *Revista Tempo, 17*(34), 45–52. https://doi.org/10.5533/TEM-1980-542X-2013173405eng

Grespan, C. L. (2014). *Mulheres no octógono: performatividades de corpos e de sexualidades*. M.A. THESIS (Sciences of Human Movement). Universidade Federal do Rio Grande do Sul.

International Olympic Committee. (2015). *IOC Consensus Meeting on Sex Reassignment and Hyperandrogenism*. https://stillmed.olympic.org/Documents/Commissions_PDFfiles/Medical_commission/2015-11_ioc_consensus_meeting_on_sex_reassignment_and_hyperandrogenism-en.pdf. Accessed 2 Dec 2020.

Iwamoto, T. C. (2019). *A repercussão da inclusão de pessoas transexuais no esporte: o discurso nas redes sociais sobre o caso da jogadora Tifanny*. Dissertation (Doctorate in Physical Education). Universidade de Brasília.

Jardim, J. G. (2013). *Futsal feminino e educação: o que a experiência ensina?* M.A. thesis (Education). Universidade Estadual Paulista.

Knijnik, J., & de Carvalho Ferretti, M.A. (2015). Ambivalent lives, fighting bodies: Women and combat sports in Brazil. In A. Channon, & C.R. Matthews (Eds.), *Global Perspectives on Women in Combat Sports. Global Culture and Sport Series* (pp. 253–266). Palgrave Macmillan. https://doi.org/10.1057/9781137439369_16

Lemes, L. F. R. (2019). *O preconceito dentro e fora das quatro linhas: o papel dos jornalistas goianos no debate sobre a homossexualidade masculina no futebol* [The prejudice inside and outside of four lines: The role of journalists from Goiás in the debate on male homosexuality in football]. M.A. thesis (Communication). Universidade Federal de Goiás.

Louro, G. L. (2008). Gênero e Sexualidade: Pedagogias Contemporâneas. *Pro-Posições, 19*(2), 17–23. https://doi.org/10.1590/S0103-730720080002 00003

Magrath, R. (2017). To try and gain an advantage for my team: Homophobic and homosexually themed chanting among English football fans. *Sociology, 52*(4), 709–726. https://doi.org/10.1177/0038038517702600

Monteiro, R. de A. (2003). *Torcer, lutar, ao inimigo massacrar, Raça Rubro-Negra! Uma etnografia sobre futebol, masculinidade e violência.* FGV Editora.

Pinto, M. R. (2017). *Pelo direito de torcer: das torcidas gays aos movimentos de torcedores contrários ao machismo e à homofobia no futebol* [For the right to support: from gay fans to the movements of fans against machismo and homophobia in football]. M.A. thesis (Sciences). Universidade de São Paulo. https://doi.org/10.11606/D.100.2018.tde-12032018-20540

Pisani, M. da S. (2018). 'Sou feita de chuva, sol e barro': o futebol de mulheres praticado na cidade de São Paulo ['I am rain, sun and mud': Women's football in São Paulo city]. Ph.D. dissertation (Social Anthropology). Universidade de São Paulo. https://doi.org/10.11606/T.8.2018.tde-11102018-110139.

Rosa, R. B. do C. (2010). *Enunciações afetadas: relações possíveis entre homofobia e esporte.* M.A. thesis (Physical Education). Universidade de Campinas.

Scott, J. (1995). Gênero: Uma categoria útil de análise histórica. *Educação & Realidade, 20*(2), 71–99.

Sedgwick, E. K. (2007). A epistemologia do armário. *Cadernos Pagu, 28*, 19–54. https://doi.org/10.1590/s0104-83332007000100003

Silva, J. C. A. da (2016). *Esporte e Heteronormatividade: preconceitos encontrados/enfrentados por homossexuais.* M.A. thesis (Physical Education). Universidade de Pernambuco/Universidade Federal da Paraíba.

Silva Júnior, J. A. da (2018). *Pedagogia do armário: identidade, pertencimento e apropriação do futebol por torcedores homossexuais.* Ph.D. dissertation (Leisure Studies). Universidade Federal de Minas Gerais.

Silveira, R. da (2008). *Esporte, homossexualidade e amizade: estudo etnográfico sobre o associativismo no futsal feminino.* M.A. thesis (Sciences of Human Movement). Universidade Federal do Rio Grande do Sul.

Simões, J. A., & Facchini, R. (2009). *Na trilha do arco-íris: do movimento homossexual ao LGBT* [On the rainbow trail: from the homosexual to the LGBT movement]. Editora Fundação Perseu Abramo.

Sobreira Filho, J. (2018). *O jogo da homofobia? Táticas e xingamentos nas torcidas organizadas do Ceará Sporting Club.* M.A. thesis (Sociology). Universidade Federal do Ceará.

Toledo, L. H. de (2002). *Lógicas no futebol* [Logics in football]. Hucitec/Fapesp.

Valentine, G. (2002). Queer bodies and the poduction of space. In D. Richardson & S. Seidman (Eds.), *Handbook of Lesbian and Gay Studies* (pp. 145–160). SAGE.

Volpe, A. A. S. (2018). *Sou gay e daí: a homossexualidade declarada por jogadores de voleibol – um estudo de caso.* Thesis (Master's). Universidade Estadual Paulista.

Weeks, J. (2000). O corpo e a sexualidade. In G. L. Louro (Ed.), *O corpo educado: Pedagogias da sexualidade* (pp. 35–82). Autêntica Editora.

CHAPTER 4

Homohysteria, Cultural Change and 'pseudo-inclusivity': An Analysis of Attitudes Towards Sexual Diversity in Sport Within Spain and Mexico

Joaquín Piedra, Rafael García-Pérez, and Alex Channon

THE DEVELOPMENT OF INCLUSIVE ATTITUDES IN SPORT

Historically, sport has been an area of male dominance, and specifically a site for the maintenance of hegemonic masculinity (Connell, 1995), where gender and sexual diversity has been obscured, and sexual minority individuals have been stigmatised or repudiated (Davis-Delano, 2014; O'Brien et al., 2013). Current research still identifies a wide range of types of discrimination (Herrick & Duncan, 2020; Smits et al., 2021), with people not fitting these stereotypes being influenced to remain

J. Piedra (✉) · R. García-Pérez
Universidad de Sevilla, Sevilla, Spain
e-mail: jpiedra@us.es

A. Channon
University of Brighton, Eastbourne, UK

J. Piedra and E. Anderson (eds.), *Lesbian, Gay, and Transgender Athletes in Latin America*, Palgrave Studies in Masculinity, Sport and Exercise, https://doi.org/10.1007/978-3-030-87375-2_4

invisible and silent under the weight of heteronormativity and outright discrimination (Krane & Barber, 2003).

However, given that cultures change and evolve, recent studies have revealed shifting attitudes in sport towards sexual diversity and sexual minorities (Cleland, 2018). The longitudinal study involving rugby and hockey players in the UK by Anderson et al. (2012) highlights the reduction in recent years of negative attitudes towards homosexuality among sportspeople, with certain homosexualised behaviours which were hitherto singled out and rejected by men now being accepted. In a similar vein, the studies by Fynes and Fisher (2016), Cashmore and Cleland (2012) or Crossway et al. (2019) find positive attitudes towards Lesbian, Gay, Bisexual and Transgender (LGBT) people in sport. Additionally, similar changes are evident in sport media coverage (Cleland, 2014). It appears that these more accepting climates within sport become stronger when direct contact is made with LGBT people (Anderson et al., 2016).

In understanding the complexity of such changes, and to help theorise the dynamics through which shifting levels of homophobia impact on climates of hostility and acceptance within sport, Eric Anderson (2009) proposed the concept of homohysteria within his broader theory of inclusive masculinity (Anderson, 2009; Anderson & McCormack, 2018). Defining this as "the fear of being socially perceived as gay" (Anderson & McCormack, 2018, p. 548), along with engaging in actions and expressing antipathy intended to distance oneself from the suspicion of being gay, Anderson notes that among men, homohysteria is typically manifested by fleeing from feminised behaviour, including physical contact with other men or showing signs of affection and emotion, while also maintaining homophobic discourse. Homohysteria helps to explain how gendered patterns of behaviour—both within and outside of sport settings—play out in relation to shifting levels of societal homophobia, particularly highlighting how homophobia can affect the behaviour of individuals who may not necessarily be homophobic themselves (McCormack & Anderson, 2014a). It thereby adds an important dimension to analyses of homophobia, inclusion, and social change by identifying the impact homophobia has on wider performances of gender and the construction of normative climates pertaining to the acceptance (or not) of sexual diversity.

Anderson et al. (2016) propose that, driven by social, cultural and legislative processes, levels of homohysteria and homophobia in society may change over time, such that societies may move through three possible stages with respect to these interrelated phenomena: (1) Homo-erasure, (2) Homohysteria and (3) Inclusivity.

Societies such as those in the UK, USA, Canada and Australia, which have been consistently analysed (Kavoura & Kokkonen, 2020) within studies which have questioned the persistence of negative attitudes towards sexual minorities, are shifting into the third of these stages, becoming generally (although not universally) more accepting of sexual and gender diversity (Anderson & McCormack, 2018; Cleland et al., 2018). Importantly, even within the traditionally gender-conservative cultural sphere of sport, research has confirmed these trends, indicating that inclusive attitudes have permeated across even some of the most historically homophobic spaces of these societies (Anderson et al., 2016).

Towards the Inclusion of Sexual Diversity in Sport: Spain and Mexico

The reality described above may not correspond to all developed or developing cultures. The works of Piedra et al. (2017) in Spain; Baiocco et al. (2018) or Scandurra et al. (2019) in Italy; Hamdi et al. (2016, 2017) in Tunisia; and Tseng and Kim-Wai Sum (2021) in China, suggest the need to delve deeper into the social realities of each country in order to study it properly. However, besides those listed here, there are few studies of such phenomena in non-English speaking countries.

In this chapter we are going to delve, theoretically and sociologically, into two similar but different realities of Latin American culture. On one hand, we will analyse the current status of sexual diversity in Spain and in Spanish sport. On the other hand, we will analyse the sporting and social context in Mexico, as an advanced and open society, within Latin American countries.

In Spain, as Barbero (2003) and Moscoso and Piedra (2019) point out, sport researchers have not taken much interest in the question of sexual diversity until fairly recently. In a study with undergraduate students, Piedra (2015) shows a wide range of possibilities in Spain's sporting context, from blunt rejection to acceptance of gays and lesbians. This study underlines the controversy that sexuality generates among sportspeople, particularly in team sports, with a climate of rejection of gays and lesbians often persisting. It highlights that Spanish society trails behind others where there is a climate of greater tolerance (Moscoso & Piedra, 2019).

In turn, the students explain that people find it difficult to assimilate social changes that are occurring relatively quickly, which is why the first impressions in these situations are of rejection or lack of tolerance. This first stage would be overcome, according to them, once these first moments have been negotiated. However, this change in Spain does not necessarily mean greater levels of acceptance (Piedra et al., 2017; Velez & Piedra, 2020); rather, a certain degree of respect is shown which may be largely due to a fear of being labelled homophobic (McCormack & Anderson, 2010). As such, the students in Piedra's (2015) study argue that Spanish people frequently adopt "politically correct" positions regarding gays and lesbians, while concealing their true attitudes and opinions. This is even more pronounced in the case of transgender people (Devís et al., 2017; López-Cañada et al., 2021). However, the only study conducted in Spain with a gay athlete questions this hypothesis (Vilanova et al., 2020), arguing that the athlete's coming out mirrored the experiences of sportsmen from the USA, and that despite this being located within a different culture, the theories underpinning the existing body of work in the English speaking context are applicable here (p. 34).

As George Jennings points out in Chapter 5 of this book, Mexico is a country of contrasts, with cosmopolitan cities that are tolerant of diversity and rural areas where a very traditional vision of society persists—including conservative attitudes towards gender and sexuality. At the legislative level, Mexico is among the most advanced countries in Latin America in terms of sexual minority rights, being an exception in this wider cultural environment (López, 2017). However, despite legal changes, homophobic practices are still common in this country (Baruch-Dominguez et al., 2016).

Crimes against people of different sexual orientations are very common; with many people being killed every year (117 LGBT people were killed during 2019 according to Mexican NGO Letra S) because of their sexual orientation or gender identity. According to Corrales (2015), the degree of progress in equality and respect policies in Latin American societies, including Mexico, depends on three factors. First, modernity: the greater the economic progress and development, the greater amount of rights. Second, the existence and power of LGBT movements: the greater the presence in the public sphere, the greater the legislative developments. Third, religiousness: the more religious the society, the greater the confrontation and difficulties encountered in passing open and tolerant legislation. According to Hardin (2002), Latin American cultures are characterised by long-standing traditions of religious intoler-ance, machismo and a male-dominated culture as a legacy of the Spanish conquest, partly clashing with the interpretations of indigenous sexuality held by Native American people. Despite this though, studies such as Ciszek's (2017) show the presence of a visible LGBT movement across Mexico, especially in big cities and in the digital sphere.

On a sporting level, Mexico has some of the oldest LGTB sports clubs in Latin America (see Chapter 2 of this book). However, on a national level, very few LGBT athletes make their sexual orientation public, with most of these individuals competing in minority sports (skating) or in female categories (football) where media visibility, and the public pressure this exerts on athletes, is low. There are no examples of LGBT athletes in Mexico's most high-profile sports such as male football, baseball or basketball.

Obviously, it is not possible to access this knowledge and diagnose this imbalance between social positioning and genuine attitude from a tradi-tional cognitive-affective perspective. However, the metacognitive social approach (Chin & Kuo, 2010) makes it possible to explore the assess-ment of tolerance and distinguish the executive control or cognitive style which fits the adopted social position, considering the degree of tolerance within a continuum between "non-rejection" and "acceptance", across a broad swathe of a society's population. This perspective in the measure-ment of tolerance opens its own field of reflection about its measurement in the world and culture of sport, and it also constitutes a new theoretical base for the construction of a measure of tolerance capable of discrimi-nating between tolerance (or not) executed mentally in a profound and adjusted way, as opposed to the production of a "politically correct" style of thinking which is essentially maladjusted, limited by its superficiality and with limited possibility of real application.

Inclusiveness as a Historical-Cultural Process (of Emancipation from the Patriarchal Structure)

Drawing on previous quantitative data where we compared Spanish and British athletes' attitudes towards sexual diversity in sport, we suggested (Piedra et al., 2017) an new stage within the wider frame-work of Anderson and colleagues' 3-stage model, introduced above. We describe this latter state as a stage of pseudo-inclusivity, sitting between homohysteria and inclusivity According to a micro-historical perspective, pseudo-inclusivity begins with a revolutionary change that overcomes the prevailing homohysteria and sexual heteronormativity in society. Heteronormativity is a belief that seeks to oppress and ignore any identities that exceed the strict patriarchal limits (binary and dichotomous, always under the superiority of the male extreme). As such, societies on the path to greater inclusion act to bring about change with the participation of LGBT collectives, seeking to secure the protection of sexual minorities with a new institutional and legislative framework that recognises and protects sexual diversity. It is at this point in the process where the stage that we have labelled "pseudo-inclusivity" comes into play, providing the framework, but not all the competencies, for the development of a social life that can be truly inclusive. As we have seen, this change has already begun in Spanish and Mexican society.

A procedural and constructivist perspective forces us to think about this more specifically, "moment by moment", even within the large stages proposed by the starting theory (Anderson et al., 2016) that we assume for its explanatory interest. We want to make people reflect on those first moments, when a society decides democratically to address the protection of a minority group but, logically, it finds resistance in the social tradition and in the lack of individual culture to embrace such changes and to reject all the trappings of patriarchy. In this context, patriarchal myths or discourses are developed to try and mitigate or resist changes towards LGBT equality by prolonging the stage of homohysteria in the face of increasingly prevalent inclusive attitudes and norms.

From this perspective, we propose a specific analysis and reflection on the new situation that involves the achievement of the objectives of legislative and institutional transformation that support LGBT collectives. In this sense, during the pseudo-inclusivity phase, tensions arise regarding major legislative changes, such as those achieved in Spain or Mexico. It is precisely during these changes that we find new forms of *machista* resistance to the abandonment of homophobia.

These give rise to a whole new (neo-*machista*) discourse, often subtle, which seeks to exonerate those who do not respect the new order, who minimise the importance of social rejection itself and who naturalise violence and discrimination against sexual minorities. Obviously, in the context of such profound changes in these Latin American cultures, such resistance occurs.

These patriarchal forms of violence are not always as prominent as the femicides that take place in Mexico. In the last report of the Mexican

National Citizen Observatory of Femicide (OCNF, 2018) in 2017, 1583 women were killed in Mexico. But, undoubtedly, there are many different ways of halting, or at least slowing down, the changes that a newly inclusive society must go through, knowing how to disarm through the bravery and courage of its orchestrated action (Butler, 2020). Success in this ongoing socio-cultural struggle can be a clear indicator of the transition to an inclusive society, which protects us not only from its previous *machista* tradition, but also from contemporary forms of discrimination.

Herein lies the interest of our study of the theory of McCormack and Anderson ( ), as we point out a specific area of reflection on the evolution from a homohysterical society to an inclusive society. In this process, we highlight the realism of the resistance to change, which allows us to lay the foundations for a real diagnosis of the elements that should be reinforced in a society (on social, educational, institutional, legislative levels, etc.) in order to bring about a real change of culture towards inclusiveness.

In particular, in order to become an inclusive society, the battle against the heteronormative patriarchal tradition must become real, promoting the recognition and inclusion of LGBT groups in all areas of society, which also requires a change in individual consciousness. No society can promote these changes without implementing the necessary budgets and economic provisions, as well as reforming school curricula and social education to train citizens to assume the change with determination and enthusiasm.

If this dedication, in the face of the excluding and dominant patriarchal tradition, does not take place decisively, the scenario acquires inclusive forms and dispositions, but not all citizens internalise them. The interiorisation of a new inclusive culture to give rise to a new social disposition, both on a personal level and in relationships with others, does not occur naturally; rather, it requires accompaniment and training. The lack of these inclusion efforts at all levels of LGBT communities generates strong tensions between individuals and scenarios. This diagnostically manifests itself in the actions and attitudes of resistance to change, as well as in the metacognitive imbalance that has previously been verified (Piedra et al., 2017). This study suggests that the idea of pseudo-inclusivity is a verifiable problem in the relationship between individuals and scenarios of change towards LGBT inclusion.

In this sense, we propose the possibility of identifying an intermediate state of tolerance of sexual diversity, between the end of the stage of homohysteria and the initiation of the stage of social inclusivity of diversity as outlined above. This intermediate state corresponds to certain premises involved at the end of the previous stage, such as maintaining a politically correct discourse and the non-rejection of potentially homo-sexualising behaviours. However, the general feature remains of the high social value attributed to heteronormative gender performance, particularly within the traditionally gender-conservative field of competitive sport and, in short, the incomplete acceptance of inclusive discourses and principles. For that reason, we refer to this stage as pseudo-inclusivity, where individuals adopt discourses and maintain preferred appearances related to the inclusion of diversity, but fall short of the characteristics attributed to McCormack and Anderson's () inclusive stage, particularly with respect to the acceptance that a variety of sexual and gender identities are legitimate and valuable.

Unlike previous studies (Piedra et al., 2017), we can now insist on other areas of the problem that require attention, such as the lack of competency for discerning and rejecting false ideas. Moreover, neo-myths must be reported because these underpin resistance to the model of patriarchal domination which emerges in the wake of social developments in terms of rights and recognition for women and LGBT groups. The metacognitive study carried out by García-Pérez et al. (2013) on the Spanish university population reveals the existence of serious knowledge gaps and a lack of emotional regulation capacity in the process for reasoning sexism and homophobia. In any case, previous studies on homophobia (Sabucco et al., 2013) in the field of school sport among students under the age of 9 suggest that we need to focus our efforts in the initial areas of socialisation, such as family and school.

The patriarchal social regime also entails, in these early stages of identity construction, "heterosexism as a mandate of masculinity", where heterosexuality is obligatory and any deviation from the norm is punished. This is what happens in the human relational sphere of a society that remains homohysterical, despite the institutional and legislative change already brought about by political and civil rights movements. We understand that for societies, such as Spanish and Mexican society, to reach true inclusiveness, without so much cognitive and emotional imbalance, they must address and lead all spheres of social influence with active policies in order to counteract those discourses and niches of social discrimination that remain evident today, doing so from a critical, gender-sensitive perspective. These active policies are more advanced in Spain, where visibility and support campaigns have been developed in the areas of sport

(CSD, 2020) and education (Ministry of Health, Social Services and Equality, 2015).

Other Scientific Contributions that Allow the Degree of LGBT Inclusion in Sport to Be Discussed

In line with recent studies, this paper underlines the importance of the analysis of tolerance towards sexual diversity in sport (Caudwell, 2013), because different positioning and attitudes linked to the presence in teams and sporting activities of people with non-heteronormative sexualities continue to be encountered. While many studies have pointed to improvements in the climate of tolerance within Anglo-American sport (Adams & Anderson, 2012; Anderson et al., 2012; Channon & Matthews, 2015; Gaston et al., 2018), it is also true, that there still exists within West countries a significant number of people who show lower levels of tolerance towards sexual diversity and bad experiences in sport for LGBT athletes (Hartmann-Tews et al., 2020; Symons et al., 2010).

Specifically, in the Spanish setting this coincides with the findings of Piedra (2015) and Velez and Piedra (2020) which already discerned a metacognitive maladjustment in Spanish society regarding the elaboration of a superficial and politically correct discourse, which was not internally persuasive on an individual level. The difference observed between the more inclusive British or American context and the Spanish context where cultural homophobia persists, together with a certain level of homohysteria, positively demonstrates the existence of differentiated mental processes which other studies across multiple cultural contexts have not yet been able to directly show.

Delving further into cultural differences, recent studies have tackled the progression of stages of homohysteria in Tunisian (Hamdi et al., 2016, 2017) and Chinese culture (Tseng & Kim-Wai Sum, 2021), identifying crucial elements of stages such as homoerasure and homohysteria. However, the case of Spanish and Mexican cultures does not seem to be on similar levels of development of tolerance towards sexual diversity (within sport), but neither are each at the stage of inclusivity as would seem to be the case in the UK or USA. Rather, Spain seems to exist within an intermediate stage of pseudo-inclusivity, while on the other hand, Mexico seems to be leaving the homohysteric stage and entering this pseudo-inclusive stage itself.

What we describe here as pseudo-inclusivity has been alluded to by Anderson and McCormack (2018); specifically, in responding to the critique that their broader theoretical perspective overstates the decline of homophobia, they note that "homophobia can decrease at the same time as heteronormativity and heterosexism persist" (p. 5). Borrowing Ghaziani's (2014) notion of "performative progressiveness", they identify a tendency for anti-homophobic discourse to prevail among groups of heterosexual people who do not necessarily "practice (anti-homophobic ideals) in their lives" (p. 5). This observation is an important corrective to what we believe to be an often heavy-handed and unfair critique of inclusive masculinity theory—that it is based on an optimistic misrecognition of decreasing homophobia, and that it overstates the positive changes that have occurred in societies (such as Spain or Mexico) that have become less (overtly, violently, persistently) homophobic. The data from our studies (Piedra et al., 2017; Velez & Piedra, 2020) provide new empirical insight which is useful in the context of this debate, revealing the manifestation of pseudo-inclusivity. In this sense, our data support the more nuanced appreciation of the dynamics of social change framed by recent refinements of inclusive masculinity theory, showing that heteronormativity can coexist with decreasing homophobia. This allows us to better understand ongoing negativity in attitudes towards sexual diversity without calling into question the central contention that overt homophobia has significantly declined in (most) Western societies over recent decades, opening up wider scope for analyses of how such changes affect the lives of sexual minority groups.

Thus, we believe that a specific contribution of this chapter in relation to previous offerings has been to identify the characteristics of an intermediate state of pseudo-inclusivity, characterised by what we have called partial tolerance towards sexual diversity, which is distinct from full acceptance and inclusion. This original contribution comes from having considered the construct of tolerance as composed of the bi-dimensionality of non-rejection and acceptance—constructs which have previously been implicitly positioned as continuous but in fact exist independently of each other, and should be handled as such in the future investigations of this phenomenon, especially in Latin American contexts where studies on sexual diversity and sport have not been developed yet.

CONCLUSIONS ON THE IDEA OF "PSEUDO-INCLUSIVITY"

The main conclusion of this chapter is that pseudo-inclusivity can be used as a tool for reflecting on the task that lies ahead for Latin American societies in order to achieve a socio-cultural status that could be called properly inclusive. This is a huge task, which will likely require the presence, participation and leadership of LGBT groups in instigating change across various socio-cultural spheres. Focussing on the development of large-scale social education programmes is a good idea. However, the drive of LGBT groups must continue to be supported, through associationism and participation, as a key element in moments of pseudo-inclusivity, in order to bring about the appropriate changes towards the equality that we hope to achieve—step by step, improvement by improvement—in the face of a receding, heterosexist and homophobic patriarchy. Therefore, penetrating individual consciousness and achieving inclusive societies should not be seen as an end result, but as an ongoing process.

In addition, our use of inclusive masculinity theory, a perspective emerging predominantly from research on gay men, similarly shapes the conclusions we have developed. This is not to say that our observation regarding "partial tolerance" cannot be instructive in various ways for scholarship on all forms of sexual diversity, but rather to stress that its conceptual roots lie in a theory which specifically pertains to changes in the relationship between men, homophobia and masculinity (Anderson & McCormack, 2018). As such, future efforts at evaluating differing levels of inclusivity may benefit from specifically differentiating between forms of prejudice experienced by different sexual minority groups, if not also mapping them against varied gender and sexuality characteristics and different theoretical frames, in order to measure the varied manifestations of (in)tolerance among and towards diverse groups of (sports)people.

REFERENCES

Adams, A., & Anderson, E. (2012). Exploring the relationship between homosexuality and sport among the teammates of a small Midwestern Catholic College soccer team. *Sport, Education and Society, 17*(3), 347–363. https://doi.org/10.1080/13573322.2011.608938

Anderson, E., Magrath, R., & Bullingham, R. (2016). *Out in Sport. The experiences of openly gay and lesbian athletes in competitive sport*. Routledge.

Anderson, E., & McCormack, M. (2018). Inclusive masculinity theory: Overview, reflection and refinement. *Journal of Gender Studies, 27*(5), 547–561. https://doi.org/10.1080/09589236.2016.1245605

Anderson, E., McCormack, M., & Lee, H. (2012). Male team sport hazing initiations in a culture of decreasing homohysteria. *Journal of Adolescent Research, 27*, 427–448. https://doi.org/10.1177/0743558411412957

Anderson, E. (2009). *Inclusive masculinity: The changing nature of masculinities.* Routledge.

Baiocco, R., Pistella, J., Salvati, M., Ioverno, S., & Lucidi, F. (2018). Sports as a risk environment: Homophobia and bullying in a sample of gay and heterosexual men. *Journal of Gay & Lesbia Mental Health, 22*(4), 385–411. https://doi.org/10.1080/19359705.2018.1489325

Barbero, J. I. (2003). La educación física y el deporte como dispositivos normalizadores de la heterosexualidad [Physical education and sports as normalizing mechanisms of heterosexuality]. In O. Guasch & O. Viñuales (Eds.), *Sexualidades: Diversidad y control social* (pp. 355–377). Bellaterra.

Baruch-Dominguez, R., Infante-Xibille, C., & Saloma-Zuñiga, C. (2016). Homophobic bullying in Mexico: Results of a national survey. *Journal of LGT Youth, 13*(1–2), 18–27. https://doi.org/10.1080/19361653.2015.1099498

Butler, J. (2020). *The force of nonviolence.* Verso.

Cashmore, E., & Cleland, J. (2012). Fans, homophobia and masculinities in association football: Evidence of a more inclusive environment. *The British Journal of Sociology, 63*(2), 370–387. https://doi.org/10.1111/j.1468-4446.2012.01414.x

Caudwell, J. (2013). Does your boyfriend know you're here?' The spatiality of homophobia in men's football culture in the UK. In J. Caudwell & K. Browne (Eds.), *Sexualities, Spaces and Leisure Studies* (pp. 9–24). Routledge.

Channon, A., & Matthews, C. R. (2015). It is what it is': Masculinity, homosexuality, and inclusive discourse in mixed martial arts. *Journal of Homosexuality, 62*(7), 936–956. https://doi.org/10.1080/00918369.2015.1008280

Chin, M. M., & Kuo, S. W. (2010). From metacognition to social metacognition: Similarities, differences, and learning. *Journal of Education Research, 3*(4), 321–338.

Ciszek, E. L. (2017). Todo Mejora en el Ambiente: An analysis of digital LGBT activism in Mexico. *Journal of Communication Inquiry, 41*(4), 313–330. https://doi.org/10.1177/0196859917712980

Cleland, J. (2014). Association football and the representation of homosexuality by the print media: A case study of Anton Hysén. *Journal of Homosexuality, 61*(9), 1269–1287. https://doi.org/10.1080/00918369.2014.926765

Cleland, J. (2018). Sexuality, masculinity and homophobia in association football: An empirical overview of a changing cultural context. *International Review for the Sociology of Sport, 53*(4), 411–423. https://doi.org/10.1177/101269 0216663189

Cleland, J., Magrath, R., & Kian, E. (2018). The internet as a site of decreasing cultural homophobia in association football: An online response by fans to the coming out of Thomas Hitzlsperger. *Men and Masculinities, 21*(1), 91–111. https://doi.org/10.1177/1097184X16663261

Connell, R. (1995). *Masculinities*. University of California Press.

Consejo Superior de Deportes. (2020). *Herramientas para un sector deportivo inclusivo con los colectivos LBTBI+*. https://www.csd.gob.es/es/herramientas-para-un-sector-deportivo-inclusivo-con-los-colectivos-lgtbi. Accessed 14 May 2021.

Corrales, J. (2015). The politics of LGBT rights in Latin America and the Caribbean: Research agenda. *European Review of Latin American and Caribbean Studies, 100*, 53–62. https://doi.org/10.18352/erlacs.10126

Crossway, A., Rogers, S., Nye, E., Games, K., & Eberman, L. (2019). Lesbian, gay, bisexual, transgender, and queer athletic trainers: Collegiate student-athletes' perceptions. *Journal of Athletic Training, 54*(3), 324–333. https://doi.org/10.4085/1062-6050-259-17

Davis-Delano, L. R. (2014). Sport as context for the development of women's same-sex relationships. *Journal of Sport and Social Issues, 38*(3), 263–285. https://doi.org/10.1177/0193723513520554

Devís, J., Pereira-García, S., Valencia-Peris, A., Fuentes-Miguel, J., López-Cañada, E., & Pérez-Samaniego, V. (2017). Harassment patterns and risk profile in Spanish trans persons. *Journal of Homosexuality, 64*(2), 239–255. https://doi.org/10.1080/00918369.2016.1179027

Fynes, J., & Fisher, L. (2016). Is Authenticity and integrity possible for sexual minority athletes? Lesbian student-athlete experiences of U.S. NCAA Division I Sport. *Women in Sport and Physical ActIvity, 24*, 60–69. https://doi.org/10.1123/wspaj.2014-0055

García-Pérez, R., Sala, A., Rodríguez, E., & Sabucco, A. (2013). Formación inicial del profesorado sobre género y coeducación: impactos metacognitivos de la inclusión curricular transversal sobre sexismo y homofobia [Initial teacher training on gender and coeducation: Metacognitive impacts of the cross-curricular inclusion on sexism and homophobia]. *Profesorado. Revista de Currículum y Formación de Profesorado, 17*(1), 269–287.

Gaston, L., Magrath, R., & Anderson, E. (2018). From hegemonic to inclusive masculinities in English professional football: Marking a cultural shift. *Journal of Gender Studies, 27*(3), 301–312. https://doi.org/10.1080/095 89236.2017.1394278

Ghaziani, A. (2014). *There goes the Gayborhood?* Princeton University Press.

Hamdi, N., Lachheb, M., & Anderson, E. (2016). Queen of fights: Lesbians in Tunisian sports. *Journal of Homosexuality, 63*(8), 1127–1145. https://doi. org/10.1080/00918369.2015.1117902

Hamdi, N., Lachheb, M., & Anderson, E. (2017). Masculinity, homosexuality and sport in an Islamic state of increasing homohysteria. *Journal of Gender Studies, 26*(6), 688–701. https://doi.org/10.1080/09589236.2016. 1155979

Hardin, M. (2002). Altering masculinities: The Spanish conquest and the evolution of the Latin American machismo. *International Journal of Sexuality and Gender Studies, 7*(1), 1–22. https://doi.org/10.1023/A:1013050829597

Hartmann-Tews, I., Menzel, T., & Braumüller, B. (2020). Homo- and transnegativity in sport in Europe: Experiences of LGBT+ individuals in various sport settings. *International Review for the Sociology of Sport.* https://doi.org/10. 1177/1012690220968108

Herrick, S., & Duncan, L. (2020). Locker-room experiences among LGBTQ+ Adults'. *Journal of Sport and Exercise Psychology, 42*(3), 227–239. https:// doi.org/10.1123/jsep.2019-0133

Kavoura, A., & Kokkonen, M. (2020). What do we know about the sporting experiences of gender and sexual minority athletes and coaches? A scoping review. *International Review of Sport and Exercise Psychology.* https://doi.org/ 10.1080/1750984X.2020.1723123

Krane, V., & Barber, H. (2003). Lesbian experiences in sport: A social identity perspective. *Quest, 55,* 328–346. https://doi.org/10.1080/00336297.2003. 10491808

López, J. A. (2017). LGBT rights in Mexico: Collective action at the subnational level. *European Review of Latin American and Caribbean Studies, 104,* 69–88. https://doi.org/10.18352/erlacs.10234

López-Cañada, E., Devís, J., Pereira-García, S., & Pérez-Samaniego, V. (2021). Socio-ecological analysis of trans people's participation in physical activity and sport. *International Review for the Sociology of Sport, 56*(1), 62–80. https:// doi.org/10.1177/1012690219887174

McCormack, M., & Anderson, E. (2010). "It's just not acceptable any more": The erosion of homophobia and the softening of masculinity at an English sixth form. *Sociology, 44*(5), 843–859. https://doi.org/10.1177/003803851 0375734

McCormack, M., & Anderson, E. (2014a). The influence of declining homophobia on men's gender in the United States: An argument for the study of homohysteria. *Sex Roles, 71*(3), 109–120. https://doi.org/10.1007/s11199-014-0358-8

McCormack, M., & Anderson, E. (2014b). Homohysteria: Definitions, context and intersectionality. *Sex Roles, 71*(3–4), 152–158. https://doi.org/10.1007/ s11199-014-0401-9

Ministerio de Sanidad, Servicios Sociales e Igualdad (2015). '*Abrazar la diversidad: propuesta para una educación libre de acoso homofóbico y transfóbico*'. https://www.inmujer.gob.es/actualidad/NovedadesNuevas/docs/2015/Abrazar_la_diversidad.pdf. Accessed 10 Feb 2021.

Moscoso, D., & Piedra, J. (2019). El colectivo LGTBI en el deporte como objeto de investigación sociológica. Estado de la cuestión [The LGBTI people in sports as a sociological research object. State of the art]. *Revista Española de Sociología, 28*(3), 501–516. https://doi.org/10.22325/fes/res.2019.14

O'Brien, K. S., Shovelton, H., & Latner, J. D. (2013). Homophobia in physical education and sport: The role of physical/sporting identity and attributes, authoritarian aggression, and social dominance orientation. *International Journal of Psychology, 48*(5), 891–899. https://doi.org/10.1080/00207594.2012.713107

Observatorio Ciudadano Nacional del Feminicidio. (2018). *Informe implementación del tipo penal de feminicidio en México (2014–2017)*. https://92e ab0f5-8dd4-485d-a54f-b06fa499694d.filesusr.com/ugd/ba8440_66cc5ce03 ac34b7da8670c37037aae9c.pdf. Accessed 24 Nov 2020.

Piedra, J. (2015). Gays y lesbianas en el deporte: Discurso de jóvenes universitarios españoles en torno a su aceptación. [Gays and lesbians in sport: University students' speech about their acceptance]. *Movimento, 21*(4), 1067–1081.

Piedra, J., García-Pérez, R., & Channon, A. (2017). Between Homohysteria and Inclusivity: Tolerance towards sexual diversity in sport. *Sexuality and Culture, 21*(4), 1018–1039. https://doi.org/10.1007/s12119-017-9434-x

Sabucco, A., Sala, A., Santana, R., & Rebollo, M. A. (2013). Discursos de niños varones sobre la masculinidad en contextos escolares. Un estudio piloto [Discourses of boys about masculinity in school settings. A pilot study]. *Profesorado. Revista de Currículum y Formación del Profesorado, 17*(1), 141–157.

Scandurra, C., Braucci, O., Bochicchio, V., Valerio, P., & Amodeo, A. L. (2019). "Soccer is a matter of real men?" Sexist and homophobic attitudes in three Italian soccer teams differentiated by sexual orientation and gender identity. *International Journal of Sport and Exercise Psychology, 17*(3), 285–301. https://doi.org/10.1080/1612197X.2017.1339728

Smits, F., Knoppers, A., & Elling-Machartzki, A. (2021). Everything is said with a smile': Homonegative speech acts in sport. *International Review for the Sociology of Sport, 56*(3), 343–360. https://doi.org/10.1177/101269022095 7520

Symons, C., Sbaraglia, M., Hillier, L., & Mitchell, A. (2010). Come out to play: The sports experiences of lesbian, gay, bisexual, and transgender (LGBT) people in Australia. https://www.vu.edu.au/sites/default/files/Come%20Out%20To%20Play%20May%202010.pdf. Accessed 6 Dec 2021.

Tseng, Y., & Kim-Wai Sum, R. (2021). The attitudes of collegiate coaches toward gay and lesbian athletes in Taiwan, Hong Kong, and China. *International Review for the Sociology of Sport*, *56*(3), 416–435. https://doi.org/10.1177/1012690220943140

Velez, L., & Piedra, J. (2020). Does sexuality play in the stadium? Climate of tolerance/rejection towards sexual diversity among soccer players in Spain. *Soccer & Society*, *21*(1), 29–38. https://doi.org/10.1080/14660970.2018.1446002

Vilanova, A., Soler, S., & Anderson, E. (2020). Examining the experiences of the first openly gay male team sport athlete in Spain. *International Review for the Sociology of Sport*, *55*(1), 22–37. https://doi.org/10.1177/1012690218780860

PART II

Sexual Orientation and Sports

CHAPTER 5

Conceptualising Sexuality Through the Mexican Martial Art of *Xilam*

George Jennings

Mexican Sexuality

The insightful set of essays in *The Labyrinth of Solitude,* the cultural critic and poet Paz (2004) views Mexico as an orphan: stripped of its glorified Mesoamerican past, yet simultaneously denying its mixed European and 'Indian' heritage. For him, Mexico lacks a distinct national identity, as it tries to emulate other countries while drawing upon its colonial legacy of racism, classism and machismo. Gender and sexuality are especially evident where he explains the rape and abuse of native women by Spanish *conquistadores* and later masters in New Spain. This is interwoven with the oft-mentioned, yet academically under studied cultural concept of *malin-chisma*—the revere and love for foreigners and all things foreign. This comes from the term *La Malinche* (whose real name was Marina), indigenous translator and lover of the chief orchestrator of the Spanish conquest

G. Jennings (✉)
Cardiff School of Sport and Health Sciences, Cardiff Metropolitan University, Cardiff, UK
e-mail: gbjennings@cardiffmet.ac.uk

© The Author(s), under exclusive license to Springer Nature Switzerland AG 2021
J. Piedra and E. Anderson (eds.), *Lesbian, Gay, and Transgender Athletes in Latin America*, Palgrave Studies in Masculinity, Sport and Exercise, https://doi.org/10.1007/978-3-030-87375-2_5

of the Aztec Empire, Hernán Cortés. *La Malinche* is often posited as a traitor to the native people of the land by Mexicans today and was one of the first women to bear a 'mestizo': the new mixed-race people that now make up the majority of the Mexican population. This is why Paz remarks that Mexicans are all the children of *La Malinche*.

In *México Profundo*, anthropologist Bonfil (1994) presents Mexico as a continued expression of Mesoamerican civilisation: one that never integrated with the national Westernising project developed by colonialist Spanish administration and subsequent post-Independence and post-Revolution governments. He argues that the Mesoamerican civilisation continues to thrive through its cultural expressions of diet, cuisine, family interactions, social structures, indigenous language and dress. He is critical of the attempted Westernisation of Mexico, which has continued in its struggle to become an economically 'developed' nation. Instead, Bonfil suggests that Mexican leaders and entrepreneurs ought to stress what is unique about Mexico through the revelation of its rich culture and heritage.

Beyond these classical theoretical books considering Mexico in the light of its history, more empirical investigations into Mexican sexuality have tended to knowledge on sexual identity, desire and behaviour between that of the pre-Hispanic Mesoamerican world of and the developing, industrialised nation of Mexico. Empirical research typically studies sexuality as a problem for specific sub-groups of the national population that requires educational and familial interventions. Common topics include: dealing with adolescent pregnancy (Menkes & Suárez, 2003); gender stereotypes (Stern, 2008); dominant forms of masculinity and power that influence sexual violence within an asymmetric patriarchal environment (Villasenor-Farias & Castañeda-Torres, 2003), as well as HIV/AIDS, prostitution and migrants' infidelities. Most studies regard sexuality in negative terms, in terms of dysfunctional behaviour (Sánchez et al., 2005), narratives of negative male wellbeing (Fleiz et al., 2008) or oppression and risk among homosexuals and bisexuals (Ortiz & García, 2005).

Nevertheless, studies conclude that there are great differences in terms of changing tolerance to homosexuality (Parrado & Flippen, 2010), as well as contraception and family planning that accompany migration north of the border, and the complexities of crossing it as homosexuals (Luibheid, 2002) and hence point the way to a view on Mexican sexuality from a perspective on embodiment, with the body being a fundamental underpinning of the migratory experience (see Parrini et al., 2007). Cantu, Jr. (2009), in his study of Mexican gay immigrant men in the 1990s (published posthumously), declares that as sexuality is shifting—changing over time and across space. This has questioned Catholic morality and control over desire, pleasure and fertility. Another study revealed gender differences in terms of the influences of religion on ideas about premarital sex, which explored another dimension of Mexican sexuality: double-standard beliefs (Espinosa-Hernández et al., 2015).

Indeed, the focus on the problematic aspects of Mexican sexuality overlook the *potential* to explore alternative and emerging understandings of existing as a human being within both Mexican society and the world-at-large. An alternative way to study sexuality is as a fluid concept that can be seen as a possibility rather than a problem. Adding to the interdisciplinary field of martial arts studies (Bowman, 2015), this chapter shares this view on Mexican sexuality by drawing upon a balance of anthropological, philosophical and cultural perspectives taken from the martial art of *Xilam*. From my emergent, inductive and thematic analysis of life history, interview and media data, I have taken a temporal approach to explore the broad concept of sexuality in its (1) pre-Hispanic past, (2) colonial legacy and (3) postcolonial potential. In so doing, I introduce conceptualisations from ancient Mesoamerica (through 'Aztec' [Mexica/Nahua] philosophy in particular), critiques of the colonial, Catholic and patriarchal New Spain and its negative legacy on Mexico, and the challenges facing postcolonial Mexico in forging its unique gendered and physical identity.

STUDYING *XILAM*

Xilam is an example of a native-inspired, gender-balanced entrepreneurial project. It was developed in 1991 by Marisela Ugalde, a Mexican female martial arts pioneer, to help cultivate her fellow Mexicans from the body up (Jennings, 2015), including aspects of their sexual energy and interactions with others for a utopian view of a peaceful, inclusive and non-discriminatory Mexico. *Xilam* is both a martial art and a shared human development system based on a holistic philosophy primarily derived from the Mexica (commonly known as the Aztecs). I suggest that *Xilam* may provide insights into the concept of sexuality in ancient Mesoamerica, offer criticisms of the colonial legacy in a largely Catholic, *machista* Mexico, and also stimulate ideas on how to deal with this seemingly negative legacy in a complex political, postcolonial milieu.

The backbone of *Xilam* has been established as a dynamic martial art with strikes, grabs, locks, kicks, throws and a range of pre-Hispanic style weaponry and rustic training equipment such as logs in place of barbells. However, in terms of its philosophical basis, Marisela and her team (including her daughter Mayra) are continually researching the philosophy and warrior cultures that inspired her to create the art. The core meaning of *Xilam* comes from *Dzilam*, 'to remove the skin' in Mayan. The (gradual) peeling away of the skin implies the elimination of external prejudice, judgement and labelling in order to see the deeper meaning of human life and the profound personal identity that can be fostered by a philosophically orientated martial art. Marisela and her team of instructors uphold a non-competitive ethos by the paper documents of flyers, banners and handouts given to students and prospective members, advertising such phrases as 'more than a martial art, *Xilam* is a complete human development system'.

Although based on indigenous and pre-Hispanic ideals, *Xilam* is intended to be non-discriminatory regarding nationality, ethnicity or 'race', and is practised by adults and children in separate and mixed classes, openly gay and heterosexual people, males and females in notably equal numbers, and by Mexicans and foreigners alike. It was this inclusive philosophy in a body culture akin to folk and indigenous games (see Eichberg, 1998), but one beyond a direct geographical community: foreign university students with retired police officers and seasoned martial artists with neophytes. During one year's fieldwork in Mexico City, I learned the fundamentals of the art, attended regular socials and meals with the members, passed my first grading, and also assisted with the *Expo Artes Marciales*, an annual event where the martial arts industry in Mexico showcases some of its exemplars.

Apart from the negotiation of intimate and inter-sex touch through body-to-body drills, gender and sexuality never appeared to be problematic in *Xilam*. Without a locker room, students normally changed together, and it was common to continue conversations in underwear. The theme of gender did emerge in Marisela's life history, but sexuality remained relatively absent in her interviews, email correspondences and informal discussions. In the year's fieldwork as a complete participant in classes and observer of demonstrations and public talks, I never saw or heard anything either in favour of homosexuality or decrying homophobia in Mexico. There were a few (heterosexual) couples training together, and partners were most welcome to watch and support the group at festivals.

Xilam seemed quite neutral on the topic, aside from one man walking with our parade flying the iris flag during the anniversary celebration of the founding of *Xilam*.

With the branch school's unexpected closure, I began to pay particular attention to the official Facebook group[1] in terms of the images and memes that is shares on a daily basis. I held a particularly keen interest in the comments it developed, and the articles it embedded for detailed reading. Once the website was published online, as a more stable basis of written and audiovisual data, I added this to my digital analysis, and combined this with its extensive collection of recent and archive videos on its YouTube channel.[2] Taking Bonfil's (1994) framework, I shed light on the creation of *Xilam* as a purposively developed 'invented tradition' (Hobsbawm & Ranger, 1983) for cosmopolitan Mexicans that in inspired by the underlying, still living, yet neglected, Mesoamerican civilisation (Jennings, 2016).

My first strategy was to conduct interviews to explore the historically based questions relating to pre-Hispanic views on sexuality, colonisation and postcolonial views on sexual diversity. Following interviews with Marisela and her second-in-command, Mayra, they connected me with two instructors, Andrea and José, who play a role in supporting the growth of *Xilam* and its communications with the general public. With their permission, I have used their real names, maintaining *Xilam* as an open case study, apart from those who have left the field such as my former classmates. This was pertinent considering that I wish to explore sexuality as a concept rather than as a desire and manifested behaviour. Like Delamont, Stephens and Campos (2017), I also decided to use real names of those teachers who wished to be identified, as their involvement in the project has become that of collaborators. My questions were non-intrusive and wished to understand the worldviews or paradigms that formed the basis of regarding sexuality as opposed to examining people's sex lives.

These interviews were combined with documentary and media analysis of related images and discourse on the philosophy underpinning *Xilam*. As Grant (2018) contends, documents present themselves as invaluable data resources, yet can be overwhelming—a potentially endless source of knowledge and ideas that have to be carefully managed and restricted. From my analysis of the interviews, I concentrated on three sources of documents pertaining to sexuality, gender and the body: (1) the *Xilam* logo displayed on uniforms and banners; (2) the slides of the official

'*Siete Guerreros*' (Seven Warriors) spectacle[3] and (3) images from the *Xilam* website.[4] These data are embedded in the following discussion on the past, present and potential future conceptualisations of sexuality in Mesoamerican and Mexico.

PAST, PRESENT AND POTENTIAL CONCEPTUALISATIONS OF SEXUALITY

This discussion first examines the pre-Hispanic cosmological basis of *Xilam* vis-a-vis the concept of *Ometeotl*, a key component of the non-dualistic Mexica philosophy. It then explores the clash of civilisational worldviews following a period of colonial and Catholic control and the Westernisation project. The final part looks at the possible ways to share the philosophy of *Xilam* and its related values to the wider Mexican public in postcolonial times. Together, this tripartite analysis provides of the root of *Xilam* in terms of its views on sexuality, the wider sociocultural scenario and offers an insight into the complexity of applying this in one particular project. I acknowledge that people cannot undo colonialism, but can work within the existing social structures by using lessons from the past and present to shape the future.

Re-imagining Pre-Hispanic Sexuality

Joyce (2000) notes that throughout pre-Hispanic Mesoamerican civilisation, gender was commonly regarded as a fluent potential, as opposed to a fixed category from birth. Childhood training and ritual shaped, rather than set, adult gender, which could encompass third genders and alternative sexualities as well as notions of 'male' and 'female'. Mirroring Marisela's employment of surviving archaeological evidence, Joyce reconsiders the value of written colonial texts when considering gender and sexuality: 'The long history of discussion of these textual sources has tended to deploy them primarily as proof of a highly dichotomised, normative set of gender identities and relations, sometimes represented as uncontested' (Joyce, 2000, p. 133).

Earlier, León (1990) showed that the broader Nahuatl-speaking communities had developed a sophisticated philosophy. In *Aztec Thought and Culture* (1990), León demonstrated a non-dualistic worldview that perceives the life of humans in constant motion. Maffie's contemporary work (2014) continued this project in English-language and open-access sources[5] by looking at how the Nahuatl-speaking communities engage in the metaphysical concept of *teotl* (energy). For him, Nahua metaphysics provides an alternative way to view the universe as a process philosophy in which something is always becoming something else: a fruit will drop and lose its life in order for an animal to eat and continue living, or a warrior at some point in their journey through life will lose their masculine identity and take a feminine, submissive role in a ritual sacrifice. During a talk, Maffie explained that *Ometeotl* is 'constantly having sex with itself' in a constant cogeneration and reproduction.[6]

Both León and Maffie have demonstrated that *Ometeotl* is a metaphor for all the Universe, the earth and humanity's place within them. Interestingly, all four *Xilam* instructors replied automatically to my question 'could you tell me about the views on sexuality in pre-Hispanic times'? with a near-identical explanation of the concept: *Ometeotl*, composed of two elements, *Ometecuhtli* (dual lord/man) and *Omecihuatl* (dual lady/woman). Male and female are seen being interchangeable, equal and necessary for each other. Marisela expands upon this analysis:

> In pre-Hispanic Mexico, we have depictions of women rulers and warriors. In fact, the concept of Mother Earth, *Coatlicue*, the *Tonantzin* ['our revered mother'], Tlali, is feminine. And *Tlaltecuhtli* and *Tlazolteotl*, which are the Lord and Lady of the Earth. We have *Ometecuhtli* and *Omecihuatl*, the Dual Lord and the Dual Lady. The duality is in the man and the woman. The man has a feminine part and a masculine part, and the woman has a masculine part and a feminine part. In that way, when we talk of this energy, it's perfectly distributed.

According to this philosophy, there is no supposed male superiority or fixed states of masculinity and femininity in terms of role playing and identity construction and maintenance; under this philosophy, masculinity can turn to femininity, and indeed contains elements of femininity, and vice versa. The Mexica, like many Mesoamerican peoples, believed that everything existed in a non-dialectic, non-hierarchical monism that united apparent dualisms such as life/death, hard/soft and male/female. Since 1521, during the centuries of conquest, colonisation and post-colonial development under Spanish, Catholic and later French and American paradigms, the concept of *Ometeotl* ('*ome*' being 'two' or 'dual' and '*teot*' being energy) was considered as a false god or deity. This is in part due to the misinterpretation of *teotl*, which was mistranslated as 'god' by the Spanish friars working with the *conquistadores*. Mayra lamented the destruction of this pre-Hispanic gender equality:

> The Spanish destroyed evidence of the feminine aspect: that there were female warriors, female priests...in their [pre-Hispanic] culture, they had them [both genders] at the same level. But the Spanish were *machistas*. And this machismo – I see it more of a Spanish inheritance that an original [indigenous] one. They [the pre-Hispanic people] had the concept of god as woman and man: they were a couple. From that point, we can consider that their culture was one of equity. All of the deities that they had were in couples[..]For example, *Tlaloc*, who was Lord of Rain (the masculine water from the sky), his duality was *Chalchiuhtlicue*, Lady of Running Earth Water. *Xochipilli*, Prince of Flowers (also linked to the sun), who is the Lord of Art was with *Xochiquetzal*, Lady of Beauty and Joy. There also exists information on a politician, a *Tlatoani* [ruler] who had a *Cihuacoatl* [snake woman] partner, but the *Cihuacoatl* could be male of female. This philosophical concept was within governance in terms of two energies, two points of view to rule as 'male and female'.

Mayra is an expert in Mesoamerican astronomy and astrology—subjects she has studied since her childhood. Following email communications, she later verified that the some of the 20 days of the sacred calendar are associated with particular sexual behaviours and are accompanied by two deities (male and female energies). Following our continued email communications, she provided me with a written summary of the 20 calendar symbols in relation to sexuality, which I have summarised in Table 5.1.

Mayra elaborated in terms of the rediscovery of Mexica ideals in their astrological system, which she has now offers as a service to private clients:

> With the 20 symbols, there's the lizard, the serpent, the rabbit, the monkey and the flower that connect to sexuality. It links to the emotional and psychological levels. They had those symbols defined that indicated a more pronounced sexuality, and in fact, there are symbols linked to bisexuality or homosexuality; the lizard can even change gender. Some say that they have that very identified. We now know that they [Mexica] had a preparation. Some people born to these particular signs went to the temple of *Xochiquetzal*, where they were educated to be pleasurers as '*alegradoras*', but there were also men. They had a different view on sexuality.

Table 5.1 Gender and sexual symbolism in the 20 symbols of the Aztec (Mexica) calendar

Calendar symbol	Gendered concepts	Sexual meaning
ZIPACTLI (crocodile)	TONACATECUHTLI (Lord of Sustenance) TONACACIHUATL (Lady of Sustenance)	
EHECATL (wind)	QUETZALCOATL (Feathered or Sacred Snake) Morning Venus	One of the principal energies
CALLI (house)	TEPEYOLTLI (Heart of Mountain) that rules the force of animal kingdom the female principle of Tezcatlipoca ("Smoking Mirror") as the ruler of the forces of cosmos	
CUEZPALLIN (lizard)	HUEHUECOYOTL (the Old Coyote) the trickster, the inventor of music and dance	Related to joy and pleasure as Xochiquetzal and Xochipilli
COATL (serpent)	CHALCHIUHTLICUE (Lady of Snakes Skirt) rules the water as the seas, rivers, cenotes, and waterfalls TLALOC (Lord of Rain and Thunder) rules the sky's water as rain and storms	
MIQUIZTLI (death)	TECUCISTECATL (who has the sea shell) is the male principle of moon energy MAYAHUEL (Lady of Maguey) female moon energy but also related to the earth	
MAZATL (deer)	TLALOC (Lord of Rain and Thunder) rules the sky water as rain and storms	One of the principal energies
TOCHTLI (rabbit)	MAYAHUEL (Lady of Maguey), moon energy but also related to the earth	
ATL (water)	XIUHTECUHTLI (Lord of Fire), celestial or cosmic fire	One of the principal energies
ITZCUINTLI (dog)	MICTLANTECUHTLI (Lord of Death) rules the underworld with MICTLANCIHUATL (Lady of Death) she carries the dead to the underworld; also, she can plead to extend life or heal the sick	

(continued)

Table 5.1   (continued)

Calendar symbol	Gendered concepts	Sexual meaning
OZOMATLI (monkey)	XOCHIPILLI (Prince of Flowers) also link to the sun, who is the Lord of Arts	Linked to the ecstasy of joy through the body; you can see the sculpture of him showing his skin full of hallucinogenic flower
MALINALLI (herb or grass)	PANTECATL (Lord of Transformation) male principle of earth, related to MAYAHUEL (Lady of Maguey)	
ACATL (sugar cane)	TEZCATLIPOCA ("Lord of the Smoking Mirror") as the ruler of the forces of cosmos and mind duality on earth to TEPEYOLOTLI (Heart of Mountain)	One of the principal energies
OCELOTL (jaguar)	TLAZOLTEOTL ("Lady of Love and Birth") another advocacy of earth energy also known as the filth eater	She forgave sins, particularly sexual sins or issues; her figure was used as a sin confessor, eating it and transforming it through the earth
CUAUHTLI (eagle)	XIPETOTEC (Lord of Time and Renovation, "the one who peels the skin")	One of the principal energies, linked to cosmos and earth cycles, energy of transformation in many aspects
COZCACUAUHTLI (buzzard)	ITZPAPALOTL ("Obsidian Butterfly") linked to the underworld and night, has jaw bone as MICTLANTECUHTLI and MICTLANCIHUATL, but also to the obsidian volcanic stone that has to be with the earth fire, the deep transformation of energies, linked to the hipbones and duality of QUETZALPAPALOTL ("the Sacred Butterfly") linked to the sacred warriors and the main worship of QUETZALCOATL concept	
OLLIN (earthquake or movement)	XOLOTL ("the underworld dog", QUETZALCOATL's twin) night Venus, linked to the underworld, the subconscious, the Ollin is the union of the two energies male, female, magnetic, electric, light and dark, and the centre or vacuum	

(continued)

Table 5.1 (continued)

Calendar symbol	Gendered concepts	Sexual meaning
TECPATL (Flintstone)	CHALCHIUHTOTOLIN (the Jewelled Turkey)	Another transformation of TEZCATLIPOCA, related to pride and vanity; also, the TECPATL has a deep concept on its draw or image, it represent both female and male sexual organs from the cellular development, as an egg or cell; for the Maya, it is the number cero as the origin
QUIAHUITL (rain)	TLALOC (Lord of Rain and Thunder) rules the sky water as rain and storms CHALCHIUHTLICUE (the Lady of Snakes Skirt) rules the water as the seas, rivers, cenotes and waterfalls	One of the principal energies
XOCHITL (flower)	XOCHIQUETZAL (Lady of Art and Beauty) duality of XOCHIPILLI, flower sign with both male and female principles	In popular language, losing the virginity is call deflowering

The leaders of *Xilam* have opted to resist turning the art into a religion or connecting to a religion. Mayra explained that the deities are really archetypes that structure thought as well as physical, emotional and sexual behaviour. So rather than looking at Mexica religion, the *Xilam* community embraces a Mexica philosophy. This is especially evident when dealing with the black and white *Xilam* logo and its relation to the interconnected concepts of *Ollin* (movement in Nahuatl) and *Ometeotl* ('force of duality') seen below (Fig. 5.1):

On middle white circle, there are two crosses: Upright and diagonal, which represent the masculine and feminine elements of life respectively. Within the central red circle is the black and white *Ollin* symbol, which represents constant movement and change. There is a gap in the centre, which provides space for individual identity between the opposites. Marisela shared this insight: 'The gap in the middle allows you to find what is totally unique about yourself. You could be a hard woman or a more feminine man'.

Fig. 5.1   The Xilam
logo (*Source* Marisela
Ugalde)

Following Paz's (2004) and Bonfil's (1994) overview of the complexity of Mexican culture, it is fair to state that there are many different Mexicos. The philosophical framework using concepts such as *Ometeotl* and *Ollin* is not dominant in Mexican society. They are perhaps esoteric to some, as they differ to the conventionally taught views of *Ometeotl* and the other figures such as four *Tezcatlipocas* (*Huitzilopochtli*, *Quetzalcoatl*, *Xipetote* and *Tezcatlipoca*) as gods. After one training session, my instructor, Tonatiuh, corrected my understanding that these deities were supposed to be gods: 'No – *we are* the gods!', in the sense that the gods are embodied, and that we are, as Andrés Segura (Marisela's late mentor) explained, derived from the sperm and ovule, the living representative of *Ometecutli* and *Omecihuatl*, which are continuously die in order to reproduce until our death, when they cease to procreate.[7] This biological explanation is further articulated by Marisela in terms of these *Tezcatlipocas* and the related four stages of life:

> Sexual energy is total liberty. It has no repression. When we see a newborn baby, it has no repression. It does its natural functions. When it's a little bigger, it becomes curious to touch itself, but then it's told, 'No, that is self-abuse!' And they change totally. And we have the opening of sexuality very well defined from around twelve, thirteen years of age. In fact, the two *Tezcatlipocas* [concepts or deities], *Huitzilopochtli* child and *Quetzalcoatl* youth, *Tezcatlipoca* adult and *Xipetote* senior – removing the skin, the ancient one. The *Quetzalcoatl* youth is when you wake up to your potential, your sexual potential. It's when the youth begins to move hormonally, to engage in sexual games, to move emotionally, and in this

culture, it's perfectly well defined by a Toltecan figure called 'Adolescent', who is nude. Below the belt, their body is like that of an ape. This ape is the energy of playfulness, the sexual element.

In certain Asian martial arts, concepts such as *qi* energy are utilised in a pedagogical sense (see Brown et al., 2009). In *Xilam*, the 'gods' are concepts that can be lived and enacted through the body in motion, much like the idea of practising Daoism through practising *Taijiquan* in an embodied, rather than academic, sense (as seen by Brown, 2016). They form the basis of the system and represent the cardinal points, the four seasons and four elements. The *Xilam* group is not (re)creating a religion or re-educating citizens through books, but it borrowing some of the core concepts to be reinterpreted and embodied by contemporary, largely cosmopolitan, Mexicans. In this short section, my aims were like Joyce's (2000): 'to make pre-Columbian Mesoamerica more distinct, to push at the limits of its strangeness from the Europe that absorbed and reformulated it over half a millennium'. (p. 1). This connects to Bonfil's (1994) call for research on the isolated, marginalised and overlooked Mesoamerican civilisation and culture. As seen in the next two sections, the *Xilam* community are attempting to remove themselves from the viewpoints of sexuality imposed during the colonial period.

The Consequence of Colonialism

I believe it [the pre-Hispanic era] was a very advanced society – with gender equality. By just saying '*Ometeotl*' (dual god/force), it is composed of two elements of *Omecihuatl* (dual lady) and *Ometecuhtli* (dual lady). If we put a god as a man, we are highlighting something to women. Man is superior because God is a man. They are superior to us. This was a great trick. A population follows this idea, and this has continued for many years. It would be interesting to see how things would be if they had continued like before. Perhaps that is why they achieved so many things. But the Spanish just followed one side [the masculine]. Finally, the [Mesoamerican] civilisation went through a cycle of growth and improvement. It got to a great level, and then it fell and the Spanish arrived, and took advantage of the situation. It was a cycle of day and night. The good and bad. The positive and the negative.
(Andrea)

As Andrea's insights highlight, the period of conquest and colonisation dramatically changed the Mesoamerican gender order, with the establishment of the male-dominated Catholicism as the only valid religion, the removal of power from female indigenous leaders and the rape and abuse of native women. This period of 'modernity' was also colonialisation that included process of enslavement, displacement and dispossession (see Bhambra, 2013). With nearly three centuries of colonial rule (1521–1817), a patriarchal, asymmetrical gender order was based on the infamous concept of machismo, which, like notions of hegemonic masculinity, was based on inter-relations between different kinds of men and men's attitudes an actions towards women (Moises, 2005). This is commonly accompanied by *marianismo,* the veneration of the Virgin Mary as manifested by the Virgin of Guadalupe (*Tonantzin* in Nahuatl), with mothers being greatly respected, but seen as passive and mysterious. Yet it was also associated with mixing of the indigenous with European conquerors, colonisers and later immigrants to form the so-called *mestizo* race. Andrea critiques the common veneration for the European side of Mexican ancestry:

> Mexicans, we need to recognise ourselves as Mexicans. Mexicas, Zapotec – we're a mixture, not just one race. We're not just the pre-Hispanic side. It is not enough to know your father's side of the family: you need to know your mother's side, too. Not just that one was a rapist who took everything, and the other one just allowed it all to happen. We must take advantage that we come from two cultures so distinct from one another, and not feel shame about it.
>
> Families are very proud of their European part, but no one is proud of their Mexican part. I'm not fighting against the European part. What gives you strength are these two parts. I come from these two parts. It's not just the Spanish. For how many invasions did they have before the time of the Conquest; we can't just say they're one thing. They're also a mixture. It's simply a question of acceptation and being proud. Being dignified.

Returning to Paz (2004), we can see the frustration that some Mexicans live with, bearing the fact that many of them are descended from a conquered, partly enslaved and often raped series of women. This is part of the mission of *Xilam*: to make Mexicans proud of their indigenous heritage on equal terms as their other forms of ethnic heritage. Coupled with this focus on gender is a consideration of the role of the Catholic church in the colonial control of New Spain. Mexico remains largely Catholic, although there is a growing number of agnostics, atheists and those interested in pre-Hispanic beliefs. Andrea expressed her own discontent with the Catholic system as one of social control:

> It's a system of manipulation against the masses. They take advantage of people. People aren't happy. They're sinning, and are always carrying the burden. They see everything as bad. Something is bad. You enjoy yourself, and then in the morning, feel bad. 'Damn. What I did was bad!' And the people who attend the church are very square, bitter and frustrated. They are people that chastise those around them. They're people who criticise and judge. 'Why do you do that?' They don't do it, but they don't permit other people to do things. This does a great deal of damage to society. If people are unhappy and insecure. The Church encourages people to be unhappy and insecure. It manipulates people.

Paz (2004) remarked how New Spain was modelled on a late-medieval Spain. The imposition of this religion and its implementation with native beliefs provided a basis for ideological control on specific issues such as the body, sex before marriage, homosexuality and sexual experimentation, which still continues in some rural communities. In an initial conversation, Marisela cited the case of the Muxes (a third gender), who are accepted as part of the Zapotec community (whose ancestors also inspired Marisela to create *Xilam*). Mayra also mentioned the Muxes as an exception:

> In Oaxaca, the Muxes (the third gender) – there's a group that are very open as well. They select the gender in which they feel better. Another example is the Lacandonones in Chiapas; even if they are married but feel attracted to another person, they speak freely about it and can change partners and divorce in order to be free. There is liberty. It's not that strong, the unity. [monogamy]

This group is perhaps illustrative of the sexual tolerance that Bonfil (1994) alluded to. These small, relatively unknown tribes form the surviving elements of Mesoamerican civilisation. Another surviving, and indeed revived element of pre-Hispanic civilisation as the *Temazcals*, which are the spa-like treatments that are housed in stone steam rooms. Today, they feature in the Mexican health and beauty industry, with a multitude of options in weekend retreats—often using modern technology and bathing suits. Marisela contrasted the revelation of the body in pre-Hispanic Mesoamerica with the *pudor* (sense of shame concerned with sex and nudity) instilled in modern Mexicans: 'An entire family can enter the

Temazcal without clothes. But because of the [Catholic] religion, there's the towel so that people don't see me [nude]. But there are some places where they just go in with sandals. There isn't this pudor. *Pudor* comes from a concept of sin'.

Postcolonial Possibilities

Despite these reservations, the bodily shame and sexual connotations with nudity are changing. With ideals of postmodernity comes views on postcolonialism. Whether we use terms such as late modernity (Giddens, 1990) or equivalent notions, there is most definitely a tide of change in society at large. Cyclists take to the streets in World Naked Bike Ride, and Spencer Tunick used Mexico City to stage his biggest photo-shoot of collective nude bodies to date—interestingly, in the Zocalo (city centre square), the former stronghold of the Mexica rulers of Mexico-Tenochtitlan. In many ways, Mexico City can be regarded as a postmodern city with all the characteristics of commercialism, technology and education for a megacity of its size and importance.

As shown by Paz and Bonfil, Mexico is a complex and pluralistic country: Part indigenous, European, Mesoamerican, Western, ancient and ultramodern. Since their writings, many developments have occurred, especially in Mexico City, where gay marriage and abortion are legal, and same-sex couples can adopt children. Indeed, Mexico City was touted as a 'gay friendly' city by former mayor Miguel Ángel Mancera, and it has an annual Gay Pride parade that eclipses any other march or protest in the city. Many of these policies and practices do not originate from Mexico, but are replications of initiatives set up in the Global North.

Striving to develop original, local projects, the *Xilam* organisers and their supporters wish to create an educational show called *Los Siete Guerreros* (the seven warriors) in the Zocalo. Andrea and Mayra are chief instigators of this plan, and they explained the rationale behind this spectacle. Andrea contrasted these warriors to the USA's Caucasian superheroes, and the need for an indigenous-inspired equivalent that is currently lacking in Mexican popular culture:

> Because children see and admire Batman and Superman, and like him because he's strong, and what not. But they don't know *Huitzilopochtli* and *Tezcatlipoca* [deities / concepts]; they exist in all of this pre-Hispanic culture, and if you attend the events, you can say, 'Ah, how wonderful.

It is Mexican, it's not *Gringo* [American]'. Because at the end of the day, how can you be proud of the *Chapulín Colorado* [pop cultural icon] who's clumsy, and isn't going to save anyone (laughs). And also, the wrestlers, the *Lucha Libre* and that. They don't have the strength of a Batman or a Superman. And to have male and female characters. Boys and girls, too. The female deer warrior. Because the woman can represent herself as being strong, too. We are strong, fast. Not just through fighting, but through specific forces. Dancing very well, jumping very well. That kind of thing. Men and women – since we were young, girls in the castle waiting for their prince for give them a kiss…we've taken that route.

This duo of deer warriors are shown below in Fig. 5.2, as part of the official proposal of the presentation that they are using to find a corporate sponsor:

Mayra elaborated on this ambition to express the philosophy of *Xilam*:

Guerreros Venado
Encontrar tu centro, llegar a tu corazón

En la cultura Wirarika simboliza el corazón del hombre como centro de todo lo creado, significa la manifestación equilibrada de las emociones, a su vez el venado representa llegar al corazón de uno mismo para reconocer y buscar el corazón de los demás, así mismo se relaciona con la sensibilidad. Según la cultura mexica es relacionado con Tepeyolotli ("el corazón de la montaña"), que tiene como representación los montes, cuevas y cañadas.

Fig. 5.2 The deer warriors of the Siete Guerreros (*Source* Mayra Armijo)

The idea of forming heroes – we call them warriors, seven warriors – each one represents a level of *Xilam*, and each one is an animal. The snake, the eagle, the ocelotl, the deer, the armadillo and the iguana. They work in pairs, as a duality. Quite simply for gender equity. Not all are going to be men and the others women. They exist in duality, because here there is duality. It is very marked, this duality. To reinforce this message of equity, we show that women are also strong, are also warriors; that is why we show them to be in pairs. This doesn't necessarily mean that they are related or in a relationship, but there is the male jaguar warrior and the female jaguar warrior.

Encapsulating this quote and challenging pudor is an archive photo of a demonstration in a martial arts exhibition. A female and male *Xilam* practitioner are dressed as jaguar warriors in a total sense of equality and equity: with the same shield and weapon, identical body paint and also the exact degree of dress in which they are both topless on stage for a bustling exhibition (Fig. 5.3):

Here, the duality of *Ometeotl* is expressed in both the symbol of the *Xilam* logo in the centre, the shields and in the revealing of young and athletic bodies in an overt yet non-sexual manner in which the sight of naked flesh is normalised in a post-colonial and increasingly postmodern

Fig. 5.3   Xilam practitioners at Expo Artes Marciales 2011 (*Source* Xilam.org)

society. The pre-Hispanic ideals are communicated through new forms of technology (the website and social media such as Facebook) using new and increasingly popular forms of body art that resemble warrior preparations of bygone times. This demonstrates how a philosophical concept can be analysed in a historically sensitive, cultural sense to sexuality as part of a broader worldview.

Conclusions

This chapter has explored the concept of sexuality in Mexican *Xilam* by considering the influences of history, culture and philosophy. My rationale for this was twofold. First, although initial fieldwork observations inspired me to look into sexuality in terms of favouring the LGBT movement, my further data collection and analysis revealed fascinating insights into how sexuality was understood as a concept, and how it was contrasted to other conceptualisations in postcolonial Mexico. Second, on a more theoretical level, I argue that the ways in which sexuality are conceptualised are the foundations for social and individual action, which can possibly compare or resist other sexuality paradigms.

Sexuality is thus not just about people's behaviour and the (un)intended consequences of their actions. Indeed, sexuality is also an idea, a concept, a way of looking at oneself and others, and finding individual space and identity. It is also connected to wider worldviews, such as religious, scientific, dualistic or humanistic ones. By studying specific worldviews in detail and by comparing them in different ways using multiple forms of data collection and analysis, we can find a more global approach to studying sexuality. My argument is inspired by recent calls for an open and eclectic forum for theorists from around the world (Connell, 2007)—one that questions the taken-for-granted foundations of sociology, such as terms like modernity, which have strong colonial overtones (see Bhambra, 2013, 2016; Bhambra & de Sousa Santos, 2017). I have approached this postcolonial social science by employing concepts from cultural critique (Paz, 2004) and sociocultural anthropology (Bonfil, 1994), as well as contemporary reconceptualisations of Mexica philosophy—in particular, the notion of Ometeotl (Maffie, 2014).

I propose three research streams to pursue this end. First, researchers could examine the conceptualisations of sexuality within the broad spectrum of physical cultures of specific countries by using an internal analysis of paradigmatic systems: religion, science, cultures, educational systems in a given region or nation-state. This might use a postcolonial or decolonial perspective in order to revaluate the systems of thought in a given civilisation and to question existing forms of knowledge on the topic. It could also use conceptual enquiry as well as employing a blend of data collection strategies. Second, scholars could pursue a global comparative philosophy (for example, see Maffie, 2001) by actively comparing conceptualisations between countries and across historical periods to illuminate how sexuality has never been seen as a fixed entity or shared reality by any given group of people—tribes, subcultures, countries, classes, etc. Third, scholars could connect these core conceptualisations with values (and value systems) and dispositions with actions through both a discursive and an embodied approach in an effort to explore what is said and written about sexuality, and how it is lived and performed inside and out of the ring, dojo, tatami, etc. These research streams could connect philosophy with pedagogy, pedagogy with practice and practice with policy.

To close this chapter on the concept of sexuality, Mayra has some poignant words on the importance of values—above all, respect:

> In *Xilam*, this [sexuality] has never been a problem. For example, I'm gay. It's been a theme that has become very open. I've never received an attack or anything. Nothing. Everyone's been very respectful to anyone who arrives, and this is the philosophy of respect. Precisely, it's part of normality...your preferences...is something normal and something personal...you don't need to say 'I'm so and so, and my [sexual] preference is...' No. In fact, at the last level called *Moyocoyani*, which is termed 'to create yourself', you have to create and know who you are and what you want to be. And from there, you search who you are, and you seek out what you are...in *Xilam*, all this philosophy, you have to work on yourself, to remove the skin, all the external, all that isn't yours, and arrive at what you really are.

NOTES

1. https://es-la.facebook.com/silam8.
2. https://www.youtube.com/user/xilam1320?feature=related.
3. Available on www.slideshare.net.
4. www.xilam.org.

5. www.iep.utm.edu.
6. see https://www.youtube.com/watch?v=6uaIeY-FGpI.
7. https://www.youtube.com/watch?v=GwXMc2VP9y8.

REFERENCES

Bhambra, G. K. (2013). The possibilities of, and for, Global Sociology: A post-colonial perspective. In J. Go (Ed.), *Postcolonial sociology* (pp. 295–314). Emerald Publishing Group.

Bhambra, G. K. (2016). Postcolonial reflections on sociology. *Sociology, 50*(5), 960–966. https://doi.org/10.1177/0038038516647683

Bhambra, G. K., & de Sousa Santos, B. (2017). Introduction: Global challenges for sociology. *Sociology, 51*(1), 3–10. https://doi.org/10.1177/003803851 6674665

Bonfil, G. (1994). *México Profundo: Una Civilización Negada*. Debosillo.

Bowman, P. (2015). *Martial arts studies: Disrupting disciplinary boundaries.* London: Rowman & Littlefield.

Brown, D. (2016). Taoism through Tai Chi Chuan: Physical culture as religious or holistic spirituality? In M. de Souza, J. Bone, & J. Watson (Eds.), *Spirituality across disciplines: Research and practice* (pp. 317–330). Springer.

Brown, D., Jennings, G., & Molle, A. (2009). Belief in the martial arts: Exploring relationships between Asian martial arts and religion. *Stadion: International Journal of the History of Sport, 35*, 47–66.

Cantu, Jr., L. (2009). *The Sexuality of Migration: Border Crossings and Mexican Immigrant Men.* New York University Press (Posthumously edited by Nancy A. Naples & Salvador Vidal-Ortiz).

Connell, R.W. (2007). *Southern Theory: The Global Dynamics of Knowledge in Social Science.* Polity Press.

Delamont, S., Stephens, N., & Campos, C. (2017). *Embodying Brazil: An Ethnography of Diasporic Capoeira.* Routledge.

Eichberg, H. (1998). *Body cultures: Essays on sport.* Routledge.

Espinosa-Hernandez, G., Bissell-Havran, J., & Nunn, A. (2015). The role of religiousness and gender in sexuality among Mexican adolescents. *The Journal of Sex Research, 52*(8), 887–897.https://doi.org/10.1080/00224499.2014. 990951

Fleiz Bautista, C., Ito Sugiyama, M. E., Medina-Mora Icaza, M. E., & Ramos Lira, L. (2008). Los malestares masculinos: Narraciones de un grupo de varones adultos de la Ciudad de México. *Salud Mental, 31*(5), 381–390.

Giddens, A. (1990). *The consequences of modernity*. Polity Press.

Grant, A. (2018). *Doing EXCELLENT social research with documents: Practical examples and guidance for qualitative researchers*. Routledge.

Hobsbawm, E., & Ranger, T. (Eds). (1983). *The Invention of Tradition*. Cambridge University Press.

Jennings, G. (2015). Mexican female warriors: The case of maestra Marisela Ugalde, founder of Xilam. In A. Channon & C. Matthews (Eds.), *Women warriors: International perspectives on women in combat sports* (pp. 119–134). Palgrave MacMillan.

Jennings, G. (2016). Ancient wisdom, modern warriors: The (re)invention of a warrior tradition in Xilam. *Martial Arts Studies, 2*, 59–70. https://doi.org/10.18573/j.2016.10064

Joyce, R. A. (2000). *Gender and power in Prehispanic Mesoamerica*. University of Texas Press.

León, M. (1990). *Aztec Thought and Culture*. University of Oklahoma.

Luibheid, E. (2002). *Entry denied: Controlling sexuality at the border*. University of Minnesota Press.

Maffie, J. (2001). Editor's introduction: Truth from the perspective of comparative world philosophy. *Social Epistemology, 15*(4), 263–273. https://doi.org/10.1080/02691720110093298

Maffie, J. (2014). *Aztec philosophy: Understanding a world in motion*. University of Colorado Press.

Menkes, C., & Suárez, L. (2003). Sexualidad adolescente en México. *Papeles De Población, 9*(35), 1–31.

Moises, A. (2005). Sexualidad en Mesoamérica: Machismo and marianismo. *Científica, 1*(1), 45–53.

Ortiz, L., & García, M. I. (2005). Opresión internalizada y prácticas sexuales de riesgo en varones homo- y bisexuals de México. *Revista De Salud Pública, 39*(6), 956–964.

Parrini, R., Castaneda, X., Magis, C., Ruiz, J., & Lemp, G. (2007). Migrant bodies: Corporality, sexuality and power among Mexican migrant men. *Sexuality Research & Social Policy, 4*, 62–73. https://doi.org/10.1525/srsp.2007.4.3.62

Parrado, E. A., & Flippen, C. A. (2010). Migration and sexuality: a comparison of Mexicans in sending and receiving communities. *Journal of Social Issues, 66*(1), 175–195. https://doi.org/10.1111/j.1540-4560.2009.01639.x

Paz, O. (2004) *El laberinto de la soledad. Postdata. Vuelta a "El laberinto de la soledad*. Fondo de Cultura Económica.

Sánchez, C., Carreno, J., Martínez, S., & Gómez, M. E. (2005). Disfunciones sexuales femininas y masculinas: Comparación de género en una muestra de la Ciudad de México. *Salud Mental, 28*(4), 74–80.

Stern, C. (2008). Estereotípos de género, relaciones sexuales y embarazo adolescente en las vidas de jóvenes de diferentes contextos socioculturales en México. *Estudios Sociologicos, 25*(73), 105–129.

Villasenor-Farias, M., & Castañeda-Torres, J. D. (2003). Masculinidad, sexualidad, poder y violencia: Análisis de significados en adolescentes. *Salud Pública de México, 45*(1), 44–57.

CHAPTER 6

Discrimination, Feeling of Discomfort, and Prejudice in Mexican Sport, According to Sex and Sexual Orientation

Oswaldo Ceballos-Gurrola, Jeanette Magnolia López-Walle,
Rosa Elena Medina-Rodríguez,
José Leandro Tristán-Rodríguez,
and Luis Tomás Ródenas-Cuenca

INTRODUCTION

The United Nations Human Rights Council states that sexual orientation is independent of biological sex or gender identity; it refers to the ability of a person to feel a deep emotional, affective, and sexual attraction for people of a different gender from his or her own, of the same gender or of more than one gender, as well as the ability to maintain intimate and sexual relationships (ACNUDH, 2013, p. 3).

Sexual orientation is important in the life of every human being as it defines each individual in their sexuality and attraction to other people; however, lesbian, gay, bisexual, and transgender (LGBT) people are often

O. Ceballos-Gurrola (✉) · J. M. López-Walle · R. E. Medina-Rodríguez · J. L. Tristán-Rodríguez · L. T. Ródenas-Cuenca
School of Sports Organization, UANL, Monterrey, Mexico

© The Author(s), under exclusive license to Springer Nature Switzerland AG 2021
J. Piedra and E. Anderson (eds.), *Lesbian, Gay, and Transgender Athletes in Latin America*, Palgrave Studies in Masculinity, Sport and Exercise, https://doi.org/10.1007/978-3-030-87375-2_6

99

subject to humiliation, rejection, and social exclusion; in other words, victims of the complex stigma-discrimination or minority stress (Campo-Arias et al., 2017; Stahlman et al., 2016). Specifically, these people still face multiple barriers to discrimination due to their sexual orientation, whether in the family, education, or sports environments (Doull et al., 2016).

Sexual orientation prejudice is a negative attitude toward someone because of their sexual orientation (Bolaños & Charry, 2018), these attitudes are present during the practice of sports and by different social groups (Walker & Melton, 2015); experiences such as a player's unwillingness to participate when a coach is identified as gay or lesbian, or parents' unwillingness to allow a gay person to coach their children (Sartore & Cunningham, 2009). These behaviors show the lack of inclusion and respect for these communities (Pirlott & Cook, 2018; Pistella et al., 2020). As a result, women and men from sexual minorities have stated that they are less likely to be physically active and to participate in sports teams (Mereish & Poteat, 2015). Despite changes in the attitude of society and commendable efforts to reduce homophobia in sports (White et al., 2020), the results suggest that there are continuing barriers to the participation of young people from sexual minorities (Doull et al., 2016; Lozano-Verduzco et al., 2019). However, it is not like this across the world since in a recent study (White et al., in press) found that athletes experienced acceptance and inclusivity upon coming out to teammates, so homophobic is not monolothic.

In British sport, for example, shown that among hundreds of undergrads for years in the UK rates of antipathy toward gay men in sport are practically nil (Bush et al., 2012).

Everyone is aware of the diversity of sports that exist, possibly soccer being the most popular and in which studies related to sexual orientation are identified. In Italian soccer, a context organized around men's dominance over women and the stigmatization of gay men is represented (Scandurra et al., 2019). Spanish soccer players demonstrate medium levels of rejection toward sexual diversity (Velez & Piedra, 2020). Women's soccer in Turkey presents a homophobic approach as referees' decisions and behaviors on the field are not always equal and may vary according to the physical appearance of the players (Kavasoğlu, 2021). In the UK with fans and professionals of soccer, there is a decrease of homophobia within the soccer culture, and they suggest that what is most valued is the performance on the field (Cleland, 2015);

however, agents and clubs are blamed for the lack of openness and challenge soccer's governing organizations to challenge the culture of secrecy surrounding gay players and provide a more inclusive environment to support players who want to come out (Cashmore & Cleland, 2011, 2012). Fans attending stadiums in European and South American countries present homophobic behavior, chants, abuse, and images of banners alluding to sexual relations (Kossakowski et al., 2020). As for fans attending stadiums in Mexico (ultras), they also use homophobic chants, acts of verbal violence, and discrimination especially toward referees and players of the opposing team (Ceballos & Medina, 2014). It is important to observe the growth of women in sports and sports leagues across the world and how they will face the challenge of fighting for the same acceptance and how the diversity that this adds to sports in general evolves.

Mexico is a country that has been characterized throughout its history as chauvinist (*machista* in Spanish). Verduzco and Díaz-Loving (2010) it stated that homophobia prevails in Mexican society, since most of the young and old do not accept homosexuality. Homophobia is understood as social prejudices that are expressed in the form of negative attitudes. In another study, that was conducted in Mexico City universities, Rull et al. (2013) found that homophobia scores were higher in male students, students with a conservative political orientation, heterosexual students, and students who did not report having homosexual friends. Results also showed that homophobia scores were higher in religious than in nonreligious universities.

The acceptance of sexual diversity in sport remains understudied in Mexico; the organization Orgullo Deportivo offers information about LGBT sports in the country; you can choose to participate individually or as a team by obtaining support for the promotion and diffusion of activities such as: logistics, scholarships, tournaments, newsletter subscription, endorsement, and recognition for sports events, among others.

Mexican citizens are only halfway to full social acceptance of homosexuality, with a score of 5 on an acceptance scale of 1–10 (OECD, 2019); employment discrimination based on sexual orientation is prohibited; same-sex marriage is only legal in Mexico City and 13 of Mexico's 31 states. According to the survey conducted in Mexico, 3.2% identified themselves as non-heterosexual (INEGI, 2017).

Having stated the above, the purpose of this chapter was to describe whether the knowledge of discrimination toward another sexual orientation, the feeling of discomfort in the behavior of members of another sexual orientation and the prejudice of a bad performance or a wrong image for society, is determined by the sex of birth and their sexual orientation (heterosexual vs. LGBT community) in the Mexican sports context.

METHODOLOGY

Design and Participants

The present study has a quantitative approach of descriptive and correlational character. It was a non-probability sampling type convenience, participated 367 people of various sexes and an age range of 16–55 years ($M = 22.22$, $SD = 5.15$), representing various sports in different states of Mexico.

Instrument

We used a survey on sexual orientation and sports practice designed ad hoc in Spanish language from the review of scientific articles (Movilh Joven, 2012; Piedra, 2016). The instrument is divided into two parts. The first details the socio-demographic data (age, sex at birth, sexual orientation, sport practiced, years of practice, and level of participation), and the second contains 12 items about knowledge of discrimination against another sexual orientation (5 items), feelings of discomfort in the behavior of members of another sexual orientation (3 items), and the prejudice of bad performance or a mistaken image for society (4 items); the items have a Likert response scale where 1 is *totally disagree* and 5 is *totally agree*. The results show the reliability and validity.

Procedure

For the online application, the Google Forms platform was used. The survey was sent by social networks to contacts in educational institutions, sports organizations, and groups of acquaintances for dissemination. The survey includes the objective of the study and once the informed consent is accepted, it is asked to be careful in reading and responding when indicating your opinion; finally, the time dedicated is appreciated.

Statistical Analysis

The data were processed by the statistical program SPSS version 24. Descriptive statistics and correlations were analyzed, as well as the Exploratory Factor Analysis (EFA) using the Kaiser-Meyer Olkin KMO correlation matrix and Bartlett's sphericity test, by the main component extraction method, using a Varimax orthogonal rotation criterion. The reliability of the instrument was calculated through Cronbach's Alpha coefficient.

For the differential analysis two methods were used, first the t-test for independent samples; and secondly, three general univariate linear models, to know the degree of influence of sex at birth according to the sexual orientation in each of the factors of the instrument.

RESULTS

First, the descriptive data of the demographic variables are shown, then the validity and reliability of the scale through a factorial analysis and internal consistency analysis; and finally, a univariate Generalized Linear Model (GLM) analysis of the factors (knowledge of discrimination, feeling of discomfort, and prejudice of a bad performance) according to the sex of birth and sexual orientation (Table 6.1).

When designing a survey to determine discrimination, discomfort, and prejudice in sport according to sexual orientation, it is necessary to check its validity and reliability. Table 6.2 shows the descriptive data for the items.

To check the suitability of the instrument, an exploratory factorial analysis was carried out on the 12 items. The value of the sampling adequacy measure was adequate, with a KMO index of 0.810 (Chi-square $= 932,305$, $gl = 66$, $p < = 0.001$). Three factors were extracted: (1) Knowledge of discrimination toward another sexual orientation (5 items); (2) feeling of discomfort in the behavior of members of another sexual orientation (4 items); and (3) prejudice of bad performance or wrong image for society (3 items) and together, they explain 65.93% of the total accumulated variance (Table 6.3).

Table 6.1 Descriptive characteristics of birth sex and sports practice in hetero-sexuals and non-heterosexuals

Variables	Heterosexual		Non-heterosexual LGBTIQ	
	f	%	f	%
Sex of birth				
Male	174	56.3	21	36.2
Female	125	43.7	37	63.8
Practiced sport				
Soccer	97	31.4	21	36.2
Volleyball	17	5.5	6	10.3
Fitness activities	18	5.8	4	6.9
More than 2 sports	49	15.9	8	13.8
Others	128	41.4	19	32.8
Years practicing sport				
<than 1 year	31	10	10	17.2
Between 1 and 2 years	50	16.2	7	12.1
Between 3 and 5 years	72	23.3	12	20.7
>than 6 years	141	45.6	28	48.3
No answer	15	4.9	1	1.7
Sports participation				
Competitive	170	55	30	51.7
Amateur	117	37.9	26	44.8
No answer	22	7.1	2	3.4

Table 6.2 Descriptive statistics, asymmetry, and kurtosis of the items

Items	M	SD	Asymmetry	Kurtosis
1	1.53	1.08	2.028	2.987
2	1.32	0.86	2.923	7.968
3	1.34	0.89	2.918	8.159
4	2.08	1.31	0.901	−0.425
5	2.22	1.38	0.718	−0.777
6	1.82	1.21	1.354	0.748
7	1.32	0.88	3.131	9.329
8	2.93	1.32	−0.036	−1.052
9	3.54	1.25	−0.533	−0.595
10	3.26	1.27	−0.276	−0.907
11	2.39	1.33	0.490	−0.909
12	3.17	1.42	−0.254	−1.174

Table 6.3 Organization of the rotated factor structure, communalities, self-values, and variance percentages explained (by factor and total)

Items	F1	F2	F3	Communalities
Have you heard of any cases of emotional discrimination on the basis of sexual orientation	0.871			0.684
Have you heard of any cases of verbal discrimination on the basis of sexual orientation	0.843			0.615
Have you heard of any cases of physical discrimination on the basis of sexual orientation	0.840			0.613
A fan has made discriminatory comments to another player because of his or her sexual orientation	0.746			0.646
A player or coach has made discriminatory comments to another player because of his or her sexual orientation	0.677			0.729
Do you think it would affect the team to have a partner with a different sexual orientation		0.811		0.585
I would feel uncomfortable having a partner of another sexual orientation on the team		0.779		0.604
Do you consider a person of another sexual orientation to be a bad reputation for the team		0.735		0.754
I would feel uncomfortable giving a hug to an opponent of a different sexual orientation		0.666		0.732
I would feel uncomfortable if two partners kissed each other			0.836	0.766
I would feel uncomfortable changing in front of a partner of a different sexual orientation			0.770	0.513
I would feel uncomfortable if two colleagues were touching each other's asses while celebrating a goal or a victory			0.678	0.670
Eigenvalues	3.64	3.03	1.25	
% of Variance	30.30	25.25	10.38	65.93

Note F1 = knowledge of discrimination, F2 = feeling of discomfort, F3 = prejudice of a bad performance

Once the instrument factors have been confirmed, Table 6.4 shows the descriptive statistics and reliability (Cronbach's alpha) of each factor, as well as the degree of association between the factor factors.

Table 6.4 Descriptive statistics, reliability, and degree of association of the factors

Factors	Range	M	SD	F1	F2	F3
Knowledge of discrimination	1–5	3.05	1.12	0.86		
Feeling of discomfort	1–5	1.78	0.89	0.07	0.73	
Prejudice of a bad performance	1–5	1.34	0.76	0.09	0.49**	0.76

Note M = Median, SD = Standard Deviation, Alfa de Cronbach's reliability is located on the diagonal, ** $p < 0.01$

Table 6.5 Descriptive statistics of factors by sex at birth according to sexual orientation

	Sexual orientation											
	Heterosexual n = 342						Non-heterosexual LGBTIQ n = 58					
	Sex at birth						Sex at birth					
	Male			Female			Male			Female		
	n	M	SD	n	M	SD	n	M	SD	n	M	SD
Knowledge	186	3.06	1.15	156	2.94	1.11	21	3.32	0.91	37	3.28	1.06
Feeling	186	2.05***	0.95	156	1.59***	0.76	21	1.67*	0.91	37	1.25*	0.44
Prejudice	186	1.46**	0.87	156	1.21**	0.57	21	1.48	0.78	37	1.20	0.71

Note ***$p < 0.001$, **$p < 0.01$, *$p < 0.05$

Differential Analysis

Once the measurement variables were determined, they were compared according to sex at birth and sexual orientation. First, a significant difference was observed in two variables according to gender, in the feeling of discomfort [$t_{(398)} = 5.67$, $p < 0.001$] and in the prejudice of a bad performance [$t_{(398)} = 3.93$, $p < 0.01$], in both, the average was higher in men ($M = 2.01$ and $M = 1.46$) compared to women ($M = 1.53$ and $M = 1.21$). Secondly, only the feeling of discomfort differs significantly between the groups (heterosexual vs. non-heterosexual LGBTIQ group) [$t_{(398)} = 3.54$, $p < 0.001$], being higher in the heterosexual group ($M = 1.84$) compared to the non-heterosexual LGBTIQ group ($M = 1.40$).

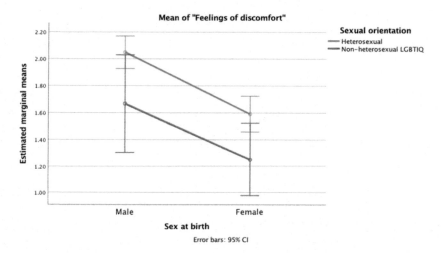

Fig. 6.1 Profile chart among estimated marginal means of feeling discomfort by sex at birth according to sexual orientation

Next, the averages of the three factors were compared by sex at birth according to sexual orientation (see Table 6.5), the results showed that in the discomfort factor, the sex at birth differs significantly in both orientations [Heterosexual, $t_{(340)} = 4.82$, $p < 0.001$; LGBTIQ, $t_{(56)} = 2.33$, $p < 0.05$]; while the prejudice factor of bad performance only had differences between sexes in the heterosexual group [$t_{(340)} = 3.08$, $p < 0.01$].

The univariate Generalized Linear Model was carried out according to the following: as predictor variables, sex at birth and sexual orientation, and as a consequent (dependent) variable, each of the three factors (knowledge of discrimination, feeling of discomfort, and prejudice of bad performance).

The results showed that only the discomfort and prejudice factors of bad performance were explained by sex at birth and/or by sexual orientation, since there was no significant explanation for the combination of both. The feeling of discomfort in the presence of sexual diversity is explained in 10% by the sex ($p < 0.001$) and for sexual orientation ($p < 0.01$). The following figure shows the results graphically.

In Table 6.5 and Fig. 6.1, we can see how the feeling of discomfort is

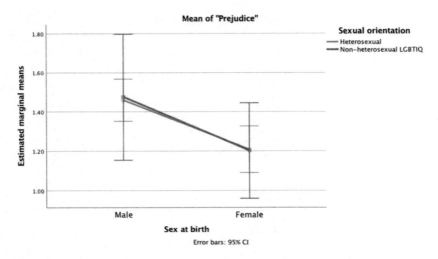

Fig. 6.2 Profile chart among estimated marginal means of the prejudice of bad performance by the sex at birth according to the sexual orientation

slightly greater for men from the LGBT community than even for heterosexual women, highlighting women from the LGBT community as the lowest average.

As for the prejudice of bad performance, it was obtained that 10% is explained only by the sex of birth ($p < 0.05$) (See Fig. 6.2), having a higher average in men from both groups, compared to women from both groups.

Discussion

The purpose of the study was to describe whether the knowledge of discrimination, the feeling of discomfort, and the prejudice of a bad performance is determined by the sex of birth and sexual orientation (heterosexual *vs* being either lesbian, gay, bisexual, transgender, intersexed, or queer) in the Mexican sports context, which was partially demonstrated.

Regarding the knowledge of discrimination toward others' sexual orientation, no differences or determinants of sex at birth and sexual orientation were found; however, a greater knowledge of discrimination was observed in men from both communities (heterosexual and LGBT community) compared to women. These results may coincide with those pointed out by Carless (2010) who mentions that, among men in the field of physical education and sport, there is a continuous feeling of otherness, since they recognize the other as a different individual, who is not part of their own community. By recognizing the existence of an "Other," the person himself assumes his identity. Furthermore, it points out that the environment with people from other groups (heterosexism, homophobia, and masculinity) during the practice of school sports makes it difficult for young people of the different sex to develop their identity, so that on certain occasions the knowledge of discrimination is not tangible.

Another study shows that most youth who identify as lesbian, gay, bisexual, and transgender, (LGBT) experience bullying in school sports, which increases the risks of mental health problems and decreases the participation in physical activity (Greenspan et al., 2017).

On the other hand, discrimination of sports fans has been studied, where men's evaluations of the athlete did not differ significantly, women formed much more positive impressions of the gay player than of the heterosexual athlete (Campbell et al., 2011). Another study carried out in soccer (Cashmore, 2011), shows that the vast majority of participants oppose homophobia 93%, and explained the homophobic abuse as a good-humored joke or, in their slang, "stick;" however, participants argue that an athlete's ability to play soccer is the only criterion by which he is judged, and his sexuality has little relevance to their evaluations (Cleland, 2015).

Based on the feeling of discomfort in the behavior of members of another sexual orientation, our results denote differences between birth sex and sexual orientation, as well as being determinants for such behavior. In both men and women, feelings of discomfort are higher in the heterosexual community, but even higher in heterosexual men. This can be analyzed from multiple angles, such as heterosexism, homophobia, and masculinity through sport (Carless, 2010; Cleland, 2015; Moral-de la Rubia, 2011). In addition, in sports contexts it is often segregated by gender, further reinforcing male dominance and its heteronormative culture (Scandurra et al., 2019). Therefore, it is more complicated for men to interact with men of other sexual orientations, first, for possible personal reasons, and second, for being in sports that, perhaps until a few years ago, were primarily male.

Finally, the prejudice of a bad performance or a wrong image for society differs and is determined mainly by the sex of birth, being higher in men than in women of both groups. Our results coincide with Baiocco et al. (2020) who in the Sexual Prejudice in Sport Scale, specifically in the prejudicial performance factor, observed significant differences between genders, presenting higher performance prejudice from men. This means that men have a greater misconception of the association between sexual orientation and sports performance. Another study on inclusive sport and physical activity among college students shows negative attitudes toward lesbians and gays (Gill et al., 2006). These results confirm the persistence of sexual prejudices; therefore, educational programs are recommended to improve cultural competence among university professionals and especially in physical activity and sport.

A worrying finding is that LGBT youth report that they avoid physical activity environments (e.g., physical education class, locker rooms, and sports fields) because they feel unsafe and uncomfortable. These feelings and experiences may dissuade young people from achieving the well-documented physical, cognitive, and social-emotional benefits often associated with physical activity and sport participation (Greenspan et al., 2019). As we remember, physical activity is fundamental to the health and well-being of people throughout their lives; therefore, continuous efforts are needed to increase participation in physical-sports activities by the LGBT community (Doull et al., 2016).

CONCLUSIONS

The survey on sexual orientation and sports practice showed adequate reliability and validity in the Mexican context, it could be a reference for future research work in a Spanish-speaking context. This scale discriminates in three factors (knowledge of discrimination toward another sexual orientation; a feeling of discomfort in the behavior of members of another sexual orientation, and: the prejudice of a bad performance or a wrong image for society), which showed differences between the sex of birth and their sexual orientation (heterosexual *vs.* LGBT community) in the Mexican sport context.

Despite changes in society's attitude and commendable efforts to reduce homophobia in the practice of physical education and sport, the results suggest that there are continuing barriers to LGBT participation in Mexico. Further research is needed to understand the factors that limit sport participation and to propose strategies that will enable an inclusive society as a fan, player, or manager of sport.

Some limitations of the study could be the online survey, as indicated in their studies De Rada (2012), Leonardo Rocco (2007), and Madge (2006) have noticed differences between the results of the measurement of the same questionnaire applied through the Internet and paper. While this difference cannot be exclusively understood as a measurement error caused by the use of a questionnaire online, it is important to note that the use of it can lead to different results compared to other survey modalities. In addition, there was a small participation of 58 responses among lesbian, gay, bi male, bi female, trans male, trans female, intersex, and queer. Then, you have people up to the age of 55, who are reflecting back decades for their results. That will skew things significantly, too.

REFERENCES

ACNUDH. (2013). Orientación sexual e identidad de género en el derecho internacional de los derechos humanos. https://acnudh.org/load/2013/11/orentaci%C3%B3n-sexual-e-identidad-de-g%C3%A9nero2.pdf. Accesed 8 Aug 2020.

Baiocco, R., Pistella, J., Salvati, M., Ioverno, S., & Lucidi, F. (2020). Sexual prejudice in sport scale: A new measure. *Journal of Homosexuality, 67*(4), 489–512. https://doi.org/10.1080/00918369.2018.1547560

Bolaños, T., & Charry, A. (2018). Prejuicios y homosexualidad, el largo camino hacia la adopción homoparental. Especial atención al caso colombiano [Prejudices and homosexuality, the long way towards the LGBT parenting. Special attention to the colombian case]. *Estudios Constitucionales, 16*(1), 395–424. https://doi.org/10.4067/S0718-52002018000100395

Bush, A., Anderson, E., & Carr, S. (2012). The declining existence of men's homophobia in British sport. *Journal for the Study of Sports and Athletes in Education, 6*(1), 107–120. https://doi.org/10.1179/ssa.2012.6.1.107

Campbell, J., Cothren, D., Rogers, R., Kistler, L., Osowski, A., Greenauer, N., & End, C. (2011). Sports fans' impressions of gay male athletes. *Journal of Homosexuality, 58*(5), 597–607. https://doi.org/10.1080/00918369.2011.563658

Campo-Arias, A., Vanegas-García, J. L., & Herazo, E. (2017). Orientación sexual y trastorno de ansiedad social: Una revisión sistemática [Sexual orientation and social anxiety disorder: A systematic review]. *Revista Chilena De Neuropsiquiatría, 55*(2), 93–102. https://doi.org/10.4067/S0717-92272017000200004

Carless, D. (2010). Negotiating sexuality and masculinity in school sport: An autoethnography. *Sport, Education and Society, 17*(5), 607–625. https://doi.org/10.1080/13573322.2011.554536

Cashmore, E. (2011). Glasswing butterflies: Gay professional soccer players and their culture. *Journal of Sport and Social Issues, 35*(4), 420–436. https://doi.org/10.1177/0193723511420163

Cashmore, E., & Cleland, J. (2011). Glasswing butterflies: Gay professional football players and their culture. *Journal of Sport and Social Issues, 35*(4), 420–436. https://doi.org/10.1177/0193723511420163

Cashmore, E., & Cleland, J. (2012). Fans, homophobia and masculinities in association soccer: Evidence of a more inclusive environment. *British Journal of Sociology, 63*(2), 370–387. https://doi.org/10.1111/j.1468-4446.2012.01414.x

Ceballos, G. O., & Medina, R. R. E. (2014). Causas y efectos de la violencia de los aficionados que acuden a los estadios de fútbol de México [Causes and effects of fan violence at football stadiums in Mexico]. *Revista Impetus, 8*(2), 129–133. http://dx.doi.org/https://doi.org/10.22579/20114680.121.

Cleland, J. (2015). Discussing homosexuality on association soccer fan message boards: A changing cultural context. *International Review for the Sociology of Sport, 50*(2), 125–140. https://doi.org/10.1177/1012690213475437

de Rada, V. D. (2012). Ventajas e inconvenientes de la encuesta por Internet [Advantages and disadvantages of Internet research surveys]. *Papers: Revista de Sociología, 97*(1), 193–223. https://doi.org/10.5565/rev/papers/v97n1.71

Doull, M., Watson, R. J., Smith, A., Homma, Y., & Saewyc, E. (2016). "Are we leveling the playing field?" Trends and disparities in sports participation among sexual minority youth in Canada. *Journal of Sport and Health Science, 7*, 218–226. https://doi.org/10.1016/j.jshs.2016.10.006

Gill, D. L., Morrow, R. G., Collins, K. E., Lucey, A. B., & Schultz, A. M. (2006). Attitudes and sexual prejudice in sport and physical activity. *Journal of Sport Management, 20*(4), 554–564. https://doi.org/10.1123/jsm.20.4.554

Greenspan, S. B., Griffith, C., & Murtagh, E. F. (2017). LGBTQ youths' school athletic experiences: A 40-year content analysis in nine flagship journals. *Journal of LGBT Issues in Counseling, 11*, 190–200. https://doi.org/10.1080/15538605.2017.1346492

Greenspan, S., Griffith, C., & Watson, R. J. (2019). LGBTQ+ youth's experiences and engagement in physical activity: A comprehensive content analysis. *Adolescent Research Review, 4*(2), 169–185.

INEGI. (2017). Encuesta Nacional sobre la Discriminación ENADIS. Principales Resultados http://inegi.org.mx/contenidos/programas/enadis/2017/doc/enadis2017_resultados.pdf. Accessed 14 May 2020.

Kavasoğlu, I. (2021). The construction of compulsory heterosexuality by referees in women's football in Turkey. *Journal of Gender Studies,* https://doi.org/10.1080/09589236.2020.186953

Kossakowski R., Antonowicz D., & Jakubowska H. (2020). The reproduction of hegemonic masculinity in football fandom: An analysis of the performance of polish ultras. In R. Magrath, J. Cleland, & E. Anderson (Eds.), *The Palgrave Handbook of Masculinity and Sport* (pp. 517–536). Palgrave Macmillan. https://doi.org/10.1007/978-3-030-19799-5_29

Leonardo Rocco, N. (2007). *La encuesta mediante internet como alternativa metodológica.* Facultad de Ciencias Sociales, Universidad de Buenos Aires, Buenos Aires.

Lozano-Verduzco, I., Castillo, C. D., & Padilla-Gámez, N. (2019). Is mental health related to expressions of homonegative stigma and community connectedness in Mexican lesbian and bisexual women? *Revista Latinoamericana de Psicología, 51*(1): 19–29. https://doi.org/10.14349/rlp.2019.v51.n1.3

Madge, C. (2006). *Exploring online research methods in a virtual training environment.* University of Leicester.

Mereish, E. H., & Poteat, V. P. (2015). Let's get physical: Sexual orientation disparities in physical activity, sports involvement, and obesity among a population-based sample of adolescents. *American Journal of Public Health, 105,* 1842–1848. https://doi.org/10.2105/AJPH.2015.302682

Moral-de la Rubia, J. (2011). Homosexualidad en la juventud mexicana y su distribución geográfica [Homosexuality in Mexican youth and its geographical distribution]. *Papeles De Población, 67,* 111–134.

Movilh J. (2012). *Encuesta sobre educación sexual y discriminación* [Survey on sex education and discrimination]. Movilh.

OECD. (2019). Society at a Glance 2019. A spotlight on LGBT people. ¿Cómo se compara México? http://www.oecd.org/mexico/sag2019-mexico-es.pdf. Accessed 14 May 2020.

Piedra, J. (2016). Escala de actitudes hacia la diversidad sexual en el deporte (EDSD): Desarrollo y validación preliminar [Attitude scale towards sexual diversity in sport: Development and preliminary validation]. *Revista De Psicología Del Deporte, 25*(2), 299–307.

Pirlott, A. G., & Cook, C. L. (2018). Prejudices and discrimination as goal activated and threat driven: The affordance management approach applied to sexual prejudice. *Psychological Review, 125*(6), 1002–1027. https://doi.org/10.1037/rev0000125

Pistella, J., Rosati, F., Ioverno, S., Girelli, L., Laghi, F., Lucidi, F., & Baiocco, R. (2020). Coming out in family and sports-related contexts among young Italian gay and lesbian athletes: The mediation effect of the "Don't Ask, Don't Tell" attitude. *Journal of Child and Family Studies, 29*(1), 208–216. https://doi.org/10.1007/s10826-019-01551-0

Rull, M. A. P., Leyva, A. H., Ortiz, F. M., Mendoza, E. P., Rodríguez, P. P. P., & Rosado, S. S. (2013). Homofobia en universidades de la Ciudad de México [Homophobia in universities in Mexico City]. *Revista Intercontinental De Psicología y Educación, 15*(2), 93–114.

Sartore, M. L., & Cunningham, G. B. (2009). The Lesbian stigma in the sport context: Implications for women of every sexual orientation. *Quest, 61*(3), 289–305. https://doi.org/10.1080/00336297.2009.10483617

Scandurra, C., Braucci, O., Bochicchio, V., Valerio, P., & Amodeo, A. L. (2019). Soccer is a matter of real men? Sexist and homophobic attitudes in three Italian soccer teams differentiated by sexual orientation and gender identity. *International Journal of Sport and Exercise Psychology, 17*(3), 285–301. https://doi.org/10.1080/1612197X.2017.1339728

Stahlman, S., Sánchez, T. H., Sullivan, P. S., Ketende, S., Lyons, C., Charurat, M. E., Drame, F. M., Diouf, D., Ezouatchi, R., Kouanda, S., Anato, S., Mothopeng, T., Mnisi, Z., & Baral, S. D. (2016). The prevalence of sexual behavior stigma affecting gay men and other men who have sex with men across Sub-Saharan Africa and in the United States. *JMIR Public Health Surveil, 2*(2), e35. https://doi.org/10.2196/publichealth.5824

Velez, L., & Piedra, J. (2020). Does sexuality play in the stadium? Climate of tolerance/rejection towards sexual diversity among soccer players in Spain. *Soccer & Society, 21*(1), 29–38. https://doi.org/10.1080/14660970.2018.1446002

Verduzco, I. L., & Díaz-Loving, R. (2010). Medición de la homofobia en México: Desarrollo y validación [Assessing homophobia in Mexico: Development and Validation]. *Revista Iberoamericana De Diagnóstico y Evaluación-e Avaliação Psicológica, 2*(30), 105–124.

Walker, N. A., & Melton, E. N. (2015). The tipping point: The intersection of race, gender, and sexual orientation in intercollegiate sports. *Journal of Sport Management, 29*(3), 257–271. https://doi.org/10.1123/jsm.2013-0079

White, A. J., Magrath, R., & Morales, L.E. (2020). Gay male athletes' coming-out stories on Outsports.com. *International Review for the Sociology of Sport.* https://doi.org/10.1177/1012690220969355

More Than a Man: Richarlyson, Ambiguous and Non-orthodox Masculinities in South American Football

Jorge Knijnik

INTRODUCTION

Seeing his 12-year-old son sad and upset about something at his school, his father approached him and said: 'Before complaining too much, think about Richarlyson.' Promptly the boy realized what his father was saying: his life was easy compared to Richarlyson's life. Richarlyson is offended and humiliated each Sunday, thought the boy—and every Monday he is back to his club, working to his limit to achieve an excellent sport performance. He is humble and gentle to everybody, never denies an autograph or a selfie with a fan, even when he is tired and stressed after a game. 'He is more than a man, he is an example' the boy wrote in his web blog.

J. Knijnik (✉)
Western Sydney University, Bankstown, NSW, Australia
e-mail: j.knijnik@westernsydney.edu.au

115

J. Piedra and E. Anderson (eds.), *Lesbian, Gay, and Transgender Athletes in Latin America*, Palgrave Studies in Masculinity, Sport and Exercise, https://doi.org/10.1007/978-3-030-87375-2_7

Who is Richarlyson?

Richarlyson is a Brazilian professional footballer born in 1982 who, during the prime of his career (2005–2010) played for São Paulo FC (SPFC), one of the top Brazilian football clubs. He was a key player in the epic SPFC squad that won three National Championships in a row (2006–07–08), the first time this has occurred in Brazil's football history. This included starting in nearly every game across three seasons of this 20-club tournament, which included 38 rounds of extremely competitive football. Throughout his time at SPFC, Richarlyson collected notable individual accolades, including the 2007 Silver Ball signifying him as one of the best midfielders in that year's Brazilian Championship. In 2011, while still in his prime years, he transferred to another major Brazilian club (Atletico Mineiro) where he won the 2013 *Copa Libertadores da America*. In 2014, Richarlyson announced his retirement from professional football. He later pulled back from this decision, and while writing this piece (2021) he still plays for small clubs in lower professional divisions.

As a SPFC player, Richarlyson typically faced 80,000 fans when playing at Morumbi, the club's home stadium. Across the six years of his career at the club, he was heavily insulted every single match by the SPFC's *ultras*, because they considered him a gay man. Though these fans cheered on his teammates as they entered the pitch, *when* it was Richarlyson's turn, supporters screamed 'faggot! faggot!', making clear their aversion to his effeminate manners. Never celebrating his on-field successes, the *ultras* also took to social media to claim that anyone who is an 'authentic *sãopaulino*' (SPFC supporter) should ask for his dismissal as, according to these groups, he is 'definitely gay'.

Football is more than a game in Brazil. Such notions are acknowledged across the literature, particularly in Alex Bellos', 2002 book, *The Brazilian way of life*. Brazilians play football in every single place, from schools, to beaches, on streets, in *favelas* or among cars, from recreational formats to organized championships, from basic to professional levels. The country stops when the national team, the *Seleção*, plays during a FIFA World Cup, including the closure of schools, banks and the courts (Knijnik, 2018). In the past few years, there has been a rise in the number of Brazilian women participating within this male-dominated environment (Knijnik, 2013a). Though this heightened engagement opens cracks within the hegemonic masculine environment, other types of non-orthodox masculinities are not yet fully accepted within Brazilian and South American football contexts (Anderson, 2005; Rojo, 2015). This mirrors the exclamations of DaMatta (1982), that football in South America should not be for all men, but for a special kind of 'real' man. This statement claims that there is no space for men such as Richarlyson, who display clothes and gestures that are not fully regarded as 'macho.' In the spirit of this claim, it is imperative that 'actual manliness' on the football realm is not interrogated by ambiguous masculinities (Benwell, 2003).

The story of Richarlyson (or *Ricky*, as he likes to be called) told through interviews, TV shows, new articles, and court cases is the focus of this study to discuss the highly homophobic environment of South American football (Abalos, 2002; Knijnik, 2015). Following this, the paper aims to open discussion about gay men in Brazilian sport, a subject which has been hidden for many years in the country.[1] Yet, Richarlyson is much more than scientific evidence; he is, as this article's introductory anecdote demonstrates, a powerful role model for young men and the whole society; a young man who performs and truly distinguishes other ways to be masculine (Rojo, 2015). By opening this debate about his life, this paper will not only inform us about Richarlyson, it will also help to refresh the homophobic Brazilian sports environment, increasing the rights for gay men who love sport but face several hurdles to practice it in the South American context.

In order to support this discussion, the paper applies a non-orthodox masculinities lens to data gathered from three episodic in-depth interviews (Anderson & McCormack, 2018; Pringle, 2018) with Ricky, as well as supplemental perspectives from Ricky's teammates, coaches, and referees who worked with him. This core data is further supplemented with participant observation with the SPFC *ultras* in their home stadium. These data were organized in thematic categories (Nowell et al., 2017) which are here discussed against a background that, while looking at the relationships between masculinity and sport, shows how sports in modern Western societies have been appropriated and used as a very fundamental tool to construct hegemonic masculinity (Connell, 1995; Connell & Messerschmidt, 2005).

Widely used in the social studies of masculinities within sports (Messner, 1992, 1997; Messner & Sabo, 1994), the hegemonic masculinity concept shows how, through the combined use of narrow and stereotyped discourses over the male body, an ideology is constructed to certify that some masculinities will acquire dominance over other types of male gender performances, as well as over femininities (Connell, 1995).

These dominant, or hegemonic, masculinities, usually contain features of orthodox masculinities, such as belittling women and any type of effeminate behavior by men (Anderson, 2005). Connell and Messerschmidt (2005) also discuss how sport, while celebrating aggressive behavior among men, has been one of the major ideological bastions to sustain hegemonic masculinity in western societies.

It is within this context that the paper asks: are Ricky's sporting life and football experiences clear evidence of non-orthodox masculinities— the ones that do not conform with the tenets of masculine orthodoxy, hence being more inclusive and welcoming of gender diversity (Anderson, 2005)? Can his football career actually be considered as a full act of insubordination against hegemonic masculinities in the South American football realm? What are the outcomes of the tensions between the incorporation and the oppression of Ricky's masculinity(ies) by the higher status' (hegemonic) masculinities within football (Connell & Messerschmidt, 2005)? These queries build on the concept of 'fluid masculinities' within Brazilian dressage as previously presented by the author (Knijnik, 2013b); masculinities which can change according to their environment and present a profusion of meanings. As football is such a prominent sport in the country, it is important to ask whether non-orthodox and ambiguous masculinities can coexist with orthodox hegemonic masculinities without being subservient to them within the high-visible context of Brazilian football.

Key Concepts

Homosociability

The notion of homosociability, developed in Eve Kosofsky Sedgwick's (1985) contemporary classic *Between men: English literature and male homosocial desire*, is a crucial concept underpinning this particular research as well as the specific field of football in Brazil and Latin America. Few contemporary social contexts have emphasized homosociability as well as competitive sports. Historically, sports settings have enabled and also provided the space to the ongoing unfolding forms of homosocial interaction which, 'through its institutions, its practices, symbols, and discourses is an excellent example of an arena for the buildup of masculinity' (Terret, 2004, p. 13). On the other hand, though, the same sporting institutions and social practices enforced rigid boundaries for its enactments, leading to a configuration where a specific form of masculinity prevails as the hegemonic model (Connell, 1995). However, and despite the fact that hegemonic masculinity, as discussed by these authors, finds a fertile breeding ground in homosocial sporting milieus, it is key to highlight that hegemony only exists in relationship with other forms of masculine and feminine enactments (Messerschmidt, 2019).

As gender is a social construct, and hegemonic forms of masculinity breed within homosocial contexts such as sport, researchers have always looked at the different ways that a range of diverse expressions of masculinities and femininities interact in an array of social environments (Messerschmidt, 2019). Connell and Messerschmitt (2005) while revisiting the concept of 'hegemonic masculinity' articulate impetus for a new conceptualization of the geography of masculinities, including the place of embodiment in these new configurations. Furthermore, these authors highlight the importance of women in these changes, and the role that subordinated masculinities have in changing the core traits of the hegemonic one. They conceive masculinity not as a fixed characteristic with which somebody is born; rather, they see masculinity as performed in the social world, within people's everyday lives and practices. According to Connell and Messerschmidt (2005) 'masculinities are configurations of practice that are accomplished in social action and therefore, can differ according to the gender relations in a particular social setting' (p. 836). Whether these interactions lead to equal or unequal gender and power relationships remains to be seen in every single context, hence the importance of studying them in local, national, and global realities (Connell & Messerschmidt, 2005).

This investigation of the local reality of Brazilian football and its oppressive gender environment becomes paramount for the understanding of masculinities across the globe. Following the global trend, masculinity in South America is also enacted in homosocial contexts (Vallejo, 2018); it is most of the times demarcated by these milieus, through 'camaraderie, fellowship and intimacy often celebrated in male culture. It also includes homophobia' (Kimmel, 1996, pp. 7–8).

Homophobia

Homophobia in the homosocial environment of sports has been well researched through feminist lenses. Anderson (2002) argues that homophobia within sports is a form of resistance; a means to prevent any rupture in the rigid patterns of traditional notions of masculinity and patriarchy that stand in organized sports. According to Anderson, avoiding the 'intrusion of a gay subculture' helps to maintain the powerful ideologies of hegemonic masculinity in this environment (p. 861). Coad (2008) sustains that the sports arena still has a 'lack of tolerance concerning nonnormative sexualities, and a confusion between the normative and the normal' (p. 17).

Nevertheless, as Anderson (2002, 2005) has demonstrated, hegemonic masculinity has been contested in several ways across the past decades of sports. Most notably, his extensive ethnographic work across multiple sport settings in the Global North shows that the once severely homophobic sports environment has become more 'inclusive' (Anderson, 2009; Anderson et al., 2016).

Homophobia has been the cornerstone of masculinity constructs within twentieth-century sport, acting as a key element to invigilate gender enactments of sporting boys and men. Yet, by exploring the not always clear crossings between homophobia, hegemonic and alternative masculinities, and (homo)sexualities within the homosocial sports environments, Anderson (2009) has tried to demonstrate that a shift has happened since the 1990s, enabling gay men to be more accepted inside the competitive sports terrain (Anderson, 2009; Anderson & McCormack, 2018). Anderson (2009) sustains that, due to the society's increasing acceptance of gay men, 'homophobia, misogyny, violence and homosocial separation associated with orthodox masculinity in increasingly unfashionable' (p. 153). Moving forward, these key concepts of homosociality, homophobia, hegemonic, orthodox, ambiguous and inclusive masculinities underpin the following exploration in a terrain where they are yet to be discussed: South American football.

FINDING RICHARLYSON

At the time of data collection, constant media surveillance followed Ricky. Though a professional footballer, he was also an ambiguous man faced with several rumors concerning his gender and a despicable court case regarding his sexuality which we will detail in the next section. In addition, his contract with SPFC was about to expire, causing certain level of stress among his immediate staff about whether it would be renewed. Given this, getting access to him was not easy. In early conversations with Ricky's staff, we outlined the objectives of the research, yet felt that the rude nature of their responses indicated that we would not be able to meet and speak with him.

We did finally make contact with a close acquaintance who was also Ricky's friend, and she was able to mediate these conversations, explaining to him that we were academic researchers, and we did not work for any media. Lastly, and against his staff's advices and wishes, he agreed to talk to us with no previous conditions. An informed consent was kindly signed by him, as we set up a comfortable atmosphere to proceed with our dialogs. We met with Ricky three times before his training sessions at SPFC and conducted four hours of in-depth interviews with him, using a semi-structured guideline in our conversations.[2]

Our conversations with him were transcribed and amalgamated within a few thematic categories (Nowell et al., 2017). These initial categories were then compared with other data sources such as interviews with two referees who used to work in SPFC's matches and with Ricky's team-mates and coach. We also spent five matches among *ultras* doing field observation about their behavior toward Richarlyson. Our 'hero' was well highlighted by the media in the last three months of the data collection and these gave to us the opportunity to record two 90-min TV sport shows discussing the 'Richarlyson judicial case.' This material produced new and refined subthemes, which are discussed below.

'Football Idols Will Never Ever Be Homosexual': The Court Case

In 2007, the main judge of the São Paulo city ninth criminal court dismissed the criminal complaint proposed by Richarlyson and his lawyers against the football director of SE Palmeiras, a major SPFC's rival club (de León, 2012). The controversy started a few weeks earlier, when a newspaper published that a 'famous footballer' would soon get out of the closet for the whole country to watch at *Fantastico,* the main Brazilian Sunday's night TV show (Pinheiro, 2007). The storm provoked by this revelation took over all radio stations and TV sports programs. During one of these TV shows, the Palmeiras football director was asked if this player was from his club. He denied, by actually saying that Richarlyson did not play for them. As Richarlyson has never been open about his sexuality, he decided to take this insinuation to the courts. By dismissing the case, the judge's court order factually stated that:

> I see no reason for the complaint: if the complainer wasn't a homosexual, he would not be offended by that claim; if he was, he could confirm or deny it, but then it would be better if he left his sporting career, as

football is a virile sport, and it is not reasonable that homosexuals were accepted in the game, as this would create an unbalance within teams' tactics. (Junqueira Filho, 2007)

The judge goes on, citing major names in Brazilian football history such as Pelé and Clodoaldo, players who won world titles, claiming that they could never be homosexuals; in addition, he states that it would generate a 'visible discomfort to bring a son to the stadium to worry about a player's behavior and their personality disorders' (Junqueira Filho, 2007). Richarlyson's lawyers complained against Junqueira Filho's homophobic and unlawful court sentence (de León, 2012). The judge was later punished by the National Committee of Justice. Regardless, several newspapers accounts deemed this court order was a politically incorrect joke (Pinheiro, 2007). Furthermore, Pinheiro saw an inherent paradox in Richarlyson's actions, raising the question that alleging the judge was homophobic may be contradictory with his actions to prosecute the Palmeiras director for publicly calling him gay.

The first relevant topic highlighted by this case is that masculinity is always a relational construct (Connell & Messerschmidt, 2005). Hegemonic masculinity only exists as it is performed and judged by other masculinities enacted, even if inhibited or prohibited, around it (Messerschmidt, 2019). In this order, the judge builds a masculine hierarchy, constructing the notion that real 'machos' in this homosocial context reflect the characteristics of idols from the past, who brought so much glory to the country. For him, it is unimaginable that a footballer might be an ambiguous man who does not perform the real, thus hegemonic, masculinity, but rather some kind of gender fluidity (Benwell, 2003; Knijnik, 2013b).

Moreover, the court sentence reveals a potential paradox for the inclusive masculinity theory. On the one hand, it is arguable that non-inclusive masculinities predominate in Brazilian's football. This was clearly cited by a judge declaring his antagonism to any form of homosexuality on the fields in judicial order. This looks like a clear contradiction to Anderson's (2002, 2009) research that shows an increasing acceptance of homosexuality in general society and also within sports milieu. In fact, Anderson shows that homophobia—and more specifically—homohysteria is increasing in many countries, like Tunisia (Hamdi et al., 2016), while others show it decreasing in other countries, like Spain (Piedra, 2015). However, a closer examination shows that Anderson (2009) has also affirmed that the changing nature of masculinities and the inclusivity process are uneven phenomena around the world (Anderson & McCormack, 2018; Piedra, 2015). While it can be said that in that Global North countries homophobia has decreased, and further demonstrated by new laws promoting gender equality in these places, inclusive masculinities are yet to be achieved in other parts of the globe (Anderson, 2009; Piedra, 2015). In addition, this particular case reiterates the fact that homophobia was the key component for the judge to create a series of masculine hierarchies in his court order (Anderson, 2002).

Yet, Richarlyson's mere existence continues to bring ongoing ambiguity and poses a major challenge for this established gender order in South American football. This was witnessed across the data, including interviews delivered by Richarlyson to relevant mainstream media vehicles in Brazil, alongside comments made by his coach and teammates at SPFC.

Hiding in Plain Sight: Homophobia in Brazil's Football

Data compiled by the former Ministry of Human Rights in Brazil at the end of 2018, shows that between 2011 and 2018, 4422 people were killed in Brazil for homophobic reasons. That means an average of 552 murders motivated by homophobia per year in the country in the past decade (Prete Sobrinho, 2019). In a study that employed a more sophisticated design, though, Mendes and Silva (2020) point to more conservative numbers, which nevertheless make Brazil the world's most lethal country against LGBT. According to their data, only in 2018, 420 LGBT people were killed for homophobic reasons, However, both studies include numbers on transphobic murders, which somehow blurry these statistics. Despite this methodological issue, it is clear that it is against this terrifying and violent background that we have to understand how Ricky positions himself within South American competitive football.

In 2010, Ricky appeared on the cover and in the central article of the Brazilian version of the *Rolling Stone* magazine. Portrayed as a pop star in an article entitled *Against Everybody*, he never retreated from a word that he said. He affirmed that his mother was always afraid for his integrity, claiming some 'crazy person can attack you on the streets.' He understands that the football environment is really *machista*, conscious that his appearance in the magazine, using hats and posing as a pop singer, would cause controversy. Such controversy was the same polemic he triggered following his decision to get hair extensions during summer holidays, claiming he has always enjoyed long hair, similar to the Italian or Argentinean players. He had even used long hair prior to arriving to play for SPFC. However, the repercussion of this particular moment was tough on him; he declares that 'people sent threats saying they would not worry to spend 20 years in jail, but would kill me for that hair.' While he claims that SPFC has always respected him (he was publicly acknowledged and received great accolades on relevant milestones such as after completing 100 and 200 matches, respectively, playing for the club), the SPFC board pushed him to cut his hair as soon as the season restarted. Ricky complied with his bosses' advice, but at the same time remarked to a journalist that 'nobody would say anything if any other player had long hair.'

Conforming to orthodox masculinity's main code of conduct brings clear advantages for athletes (Anderson, 2009), these unwritten codes are frequently associated to athletes' gendered performances of being 'tough,' oppressing women and other subordinated masculinities (Connell & Messerschmidt, 2005). But those codes also assume that athletes will perform at their limit, or even go beyond their physical limits to prove themselves as actual men (Anderson, 2009). Examining Richarlyson's bodily and gendered enactments brings us paradoxical perspectives that challenge the notions of rigid and preexisting hegemonic and subordinated masculinities such as those constructed by Connell and Messerschmidt (2005). He clearly embodies the ambiguous man. On the one hand, Ricky is effeminate. His voice, the way he talks to people, how he organizes his personal effects; the ways he transmits his feelings and thoughts, everything around him carries a 'vibe' of a perceived femininity. This performing evidently influences and disturbs the supporters and the 'macho' football environment, bringing against him the heavy and constant war against the effeminate boy (Connell & Messerschmidt, 2005).

Yet, on the other hand, he is considered a tough man by many. His coach at SPFC confided us that 'Ricky is my bravest player; anyone would have given football up after everything he had to go through.' His experienced coach was referring to the daily insults and prejudice that surround Ricky's life. He meant that Ricky is bold inside, and that his personality is of a real man. Moreover, he mentioned that Ricky is the fittest player in the club and has beaten everyone else in the physical tests for several seasons. In order to acquire this excellent body performance, Richarlyson evidently has to comply with other norms of the hyper masculine sporting culture, that demand risking your own physical wellbeing 'for the sake of sport and team' (Anderson, 2009, p. 55). This leads to the remaining question, whether Ricky's ambiguous masculinity has really threatened the orthodox gender environment of Brazilian football.

At Richarlyson's Heart

> Richarlyson Barbosa Felisbino. I will always be Richarlyson Barbosa Felisbino, not Richarlyson Barbosa Lopes nor Richarlyson Barbosa Oliveira as some want me to be.

While discussing his own identity, Ricky asserted to us that he will never live under others' parameters and moral compasses. There were several passages in the interview that he refers to himself as being a man with a strong personality. In the third interview, as he got more used to us, he expands on the topic of his personality, as he believes his philosophy of life challenges the traditional masculine world:

> For me to be a man, this is even more shocking. Especially for the male universe and for the society that deals with football that is totally homophobic, that is totally masculine. Maybe because of my way of expressing myself with people, for my sentimental side of being, of having a very strong personality, for my side of not being very fond of saying about my personal life, this often sounds strange to the male universe. So maybe it is much more on that side it happened all these things that happened.

Without giving us time to unfold 'these things that happened,' he continues nonstop with his speech, but now referring to himself as a third person, trying perhaps to find an explanation for his suffering:

> They might be jealous of Richarlyson, not the successful professional, the winner athlete, but the man; the person who is himself, who has a strong personality, who says what he thinks looking at people's eyes, but who is sentimental; who is caring toward his younger teammates, who is loving, who likes to protect his friends, understand?

Here Richarlyson is clearly transgressing the boundaries of orthodox masculinity as he looks for different means to express his 'strong self' (Anderson, 2009). By affirming his emotional side, he comes up with a persona who is gentle and caring, who expresses his love for his friends, which, according to him, is not something that belongs in the male football context. As he articulates his life philosophy, he demonstrates fluidity in his ways of being masculine (Knijnik, 2013b).

Yet again, on the other hand, confirming the thesis of the ambiguous masculinity that he evokes, Richarlyson looks for other potential explanations of 'the things that happened' to him. While it seems he may suggest that these characteristics of caring and sentimentality are what instills hegemonic masculinity and the subsequent subordination of men such as himself through aggressive and homophobic reactions, Richarlyson backsteps from further clarification on any correlation between these characteristics and his own sexual orientation. Rather, he contemplates that it is always his 'strong personality' that is 'strange to the male universe' that ends up being caught under the orthodox masculinity's homophobic fire (Anderson, 2009; Connell, 1995).

In the last interview, Richarlyson opened up a bit to us about his romantic life and dreams for the future. However, while he talks about his own sexuality, this comes again as a dare to the orthodox masculinity that needs to disclose and broadcast its sexual feats, particularly within Latino contexts (Abalos, 2002; Connell, 1995). Ricky, on the other hand, is modest about his accomplishments on the sexual aspect of his life:

> Until I was 21, and I have no problem speaking, I was a virgin, until I was twenty-one, and that sounds strange within the male universe: how come a virgin man until twenty-one?

Again, Ricky puts himself under the ambiguity umbrella; while he acknowledges the existence of social pressure for man to be virile and perform in the sexual terrain since tender ages, he asserts his own way of being a different male within the football milieu. Will this ambiguity lead to a final disclosure about the real Ricky?

Who Has the Last Laugh?

As recently as 2017, supporters of Guarani FC, a club who once belonged to the top Brazilian teams, but now strives as a second-tier team, reacted violently against the club's intent to hire Richarlyson to fill a void in their midfield. A few supporters even dropped explosive devices such as bombs in the club's headquarters. Homophobia also exploded in the club's supporters' social media channels. Rivals would not stop mocking at them due their new acquired player and his 'masculinity' (De Vico, 2017). Despite these protests, and in a possible sign of lessening homophobia in the football environment, the coach and the club's management supported his signing, stating that Ricky was a great addition to the team's lineup and that, on the field, he would show his leadership to the squad's younger players.

These are clear signs that an ambiguous man such as Richarlyson still infuriates and challenges orthodox masculinity in the South American football context. Many men cannot support an effeminate man on the football field. They might even accept different men in other milieus, but never in their sacred male space (Knijnik, 2013a, 2013b).

Ricky's story has provoked a real crack on the once monolithic space of orthodox masculinity in South America. He not only persevered, but he was also really successful as a professional footballer. Yet, he has never stated publicly if he is gay, bisexual, or straight. If he is attracted to males, one can understand his desire to remain closeted as Anderson (2005) has shown that coming out may have negative effects in athletes' careers, such that it is a barely imagined and never implemented alternative in their career. Nonetheless, at the end of the interview, before wrapping up and running to his practice, as he reflects on whether he is a role model for other young footballers or not, Richarlyson ventures to imagine things in future:

> Maybe in thirty years' time it will continue the same thing, but that can happen and a player who is brave enough and who is homosexual and comes out. An example, as it is in my case, that happened people judging you and wanting to stereotype you as a person you are not; maybe my example could be this and I can say for those people who may be homosexuals and like to play football that if you respect other people's limits and do not invade their private life, you can win in any area in your life. Of course you always have to be you.

As researchers, we cannot say whether Richarlyson is homosexual or not. Perhaps Richarlyson needs more time, such as the thirty years he predicted above, to deal with the challenges of coming out. Yet, this is not the point of this paper. The central argument that is illuminated by Ricky's sporting trajectory is that his ambiguous masculinity won over orthodox masculinity within the environment he worked in. Despite enacting some characteristics of a sporting orthodox masculinity, such as being super fit, Ricky has never bended over toward the philosophical tenets of gender hegemony; his presence and his gender performance continuously challenged hegemonic masculinity within Brazilian football fields, transforming him in a great role model, as the father was pointing out to his son at the beginning of this article.

As recent as in 2019, football clubs in South America started to be punished by the South American football federation (CONMEBOL) with fines and points losses for the homophobic behavior of their supporters on the stands. Slowly, a 'tradition' of screaming 'faggot' toward goalkeepers who prepare to take a goal kick is disappearing from the subcontinent's football stadiums.

It looks like Ricky is having the last laugh.

NOTES

1. As far as I know, the only high-level Brazilian man athlete who came out was a volleyball player, Lilico, who played as a professional during the 80s and 90s and passed away in 2007. Lilico used to say that his homosexuality was the main reason why he has been never called for the highly successful Brazilian National Volleyball Team.
2. A big thanks to my former students and great friends Neilton Ferreira Jr and Paulo Falcão-Defino for their great work with these interviews; also I would like to express my gratitude to Alex Richmond for her careful language editing of this article.

REFERENCES

Abalos, D. T. (2002). *The Latino male: A radical redefinition*. Lynne Rienner Press.
Anderson, E. (2002). Openly gay athletes: Contesting hegemonic masculinity in a homophobic environment. *Gender & Society, 16*(6), 860–877.

Anderson, E. (2005). Orthodox and inclusive masculinity: Competing masculinities among heterosexual men in a feminized terrain. *Sociological Perspectives, 48*(3), 337–355. https://doi.org/10.1177/089124302237892

Anderson, E. (2009). *Inclusive masculinity: The changing nature of masculinities.* Routledge.

Anderson, E., Magrath, R., & Bullingham, R. (2016). *Out in sport: The experiences of openly gay and lesbian athletes in competitive sport.* Routledge.

Anderson, E., & McCormack, M. (2018). Inclusive masculinity theory: Overview, reflection and refinement. *Journal of Gender Studies, 27*(5), 547–561. https://doi.org/10.1080/09589236.2016.1245605

Bellos, A. (2002). *Futebol, the Brazilian way of life.* Bloomsburry.

Benwell, B. (2003). Ambiguous masculinities: Heroism and anti-heroism in the men's lifestyle magazine. *The Sociological Review, 51*(1), 151–168. https://doi.org/10.1111/j.1467-954X.2003.tb03609.x

Coad, D. (2008). *The metrosexual: gender, sexuality, and sport.* SUNY Press.

Connell, R. (1995). *Masculinities.* Allen & Unwin.

Connell, R., & Messerschmidt, J. (2005). Hegemonic masculinity – Rethinking the concept. *Gender & Society, 19*(6), 829–857. https://doi.org/10.1177/0891243205278639

DaMatta, R. (1982). Esporte na Sociedade: Um Ensaio sobre o Futebol Brasileiro. In R. DaMatta (Ed.), *Universo do Futebol: Esporte e Sociedade Brasileira* (pp. 19–42). Edições Pinakotheke.

de León, A. (2012). A bola e a caneta: Discursos sexistas numa sentença judicial [The ball and the pen: Sexist discourses in a court judgment]. *Redisco, 1*(1), 7–16.

De Vico, M. (2017). Caso Richarlyson: futebol é tão preconceituoso que nem reconhece homofobia. https://www.uol.com.br/esporte/futebol/ultimas-noticias/2017/05/11/caso-richarlyson-futebol-e-tao-homofobico-que-nem-reconhece-sua-homofobia.htm. Accessed 24 Aug 2018.

Hamdi, N., Lachheb, M., & Anderson, E. (2016). Queen of fights: Lesbians in Tunisian sports. *Journal of Homosexuality, 63*(8), 1127–1145. https://doi.org/10.1080/00918369.2015.1117902

Junqueira Filho, M. M. (2007). Court order number 936/07.

Kimmel, M. (1996). *Manhood in America: a cultural history.* The Free Press.

Knijnik, J. (2013a). Visions of gender justice untested feasibility on the football fields of Brazil. *Journal of Sport & Social Issues, 37*(1), 8–30. https://doi.org/10.1177/0193723512455924

Knijnik, J. (2013b). The black, the white, the green: Fluid masculinities in Brazilian dressage. In M. Adelman & J. Knijnik (Eds.), *Gender and equestrian sport: Riding around the world* (pp. 183–194). Springer.

Knijnik, J. (2015). Femininities and masculinities in Brazilian women's football: Resistance and compliance. *Journal of International Women's Studies, 16*(3), 54–70.

Knijnik, J. (2018). *The World Cup Chronicles: 31 days that rocked Brazil*. Fair Play Publishing.

Mendes, W. G., & Silva, C. M. F.P.(2020). Homicídios da População de Lésbicas, Gays, Bissexuais, Travestis, Transexuais ou Transgêneros (LGBT) no Brasil: uma Análise Espacial. *Ciência & Saúde Coletiva, 25*(5), 1709–1722. https://doi.org/10.1590/1413-81232020255.33672019

Messerschmidt, J. W. (2019). The salience of "hegemonic masculinity." *Men and Masculinities, 22*(1), 85–91. https://doi.org/10.1177/1097184X18805555

Messner, M. (1992). *Power at play: sports and the problem of masculinity*. Beacon Press

Messner, M. (1997). *Politics of masculinities: men in movements*. Sage Publications.

Messner, M., & Sabo, D. (1994). *Sex, violence & power in sports: Rethinking masculinity*. Crossing Press.

Nowell, L. S., Norris, J. M., White, D. E., & Moules, N. J. (2017). Thematic analysis: Striving to meet the trustworthiness criteria. *International Journal of Qualitative Methods, 16*(1), 1–13. https://doi.org/10.1177/1609406917773847

Piedra, J. (2015). Gays y lesbianas en el deporte: discurso de jóvenes universitarios españoles en torno a su aceptación [Gays and lesbians in sport. University students' discourse on their acceptance]. *Movimento, 21*(4), 1067–1081.

Pinheiro, A. (2007). Juiz nega ação de Richarlyson e diz que futebol é para macho. 3 August. https://www.conjur.com.br/2007-ago-03/juiz_nega_acao_jogador_futebol_macho. Accessed 11 Jul 2009.

Prete Sobrinho, W. (2019). Brasil registra uma morte por homofobia a cada 16 horas, aponta relatório. https://noticias.uol.com.br/cotidiano/ultimas-noticias/2019/02/20/brasil-matou-8-mil-lgbt-desde-1963-governo-dificulta-divulgacao-de-dados.htm. Accessed 20 Feb 2021.

Pringle, R. (2018). On the development of sport and masculinities research: Feminism as a discourse of inspiration and theoretical legitimation. In L. Mansfield, J. Caudwell, B. Wheaton, & B. Waston (Eds.), *The Palgrave handbook of feminism and sport, leisure and physical education* (pp. 73–93). Palgrave Macmillan.

Rojo, L. (2015). "Other" Masculinities: Equestrianism in Uruguay. In J. Knijnik & D. Adair (Eds.), *Embodied masculinities in global sport* (pp. 53–70). FIT.

Sedgwick, E. K. (1985). *Between men: English literature and male homosocial desire*. Columbia University Press.

Terret, T. (2004). Sport et Masculinité: une revue de questions [Sport and Masculinity: a review of issues]. *Revue International des sciences du sport et de l'éducation physique (Spécial Activités Physiques et Genre)*, *66*, 209–225.

Vallejo, G. (2018). El hombre nuevo: Representaciones culturales en torno a la masculinidad en la Argentina (1918–1976) [The New Man: Cultural strategies around masculinity in Argentina (1918–1976)]. *Cuadernos De Historia Contemporánea*, *40*, 89–113. https://doi.org/10.5209/CHCO.60324

CHAPTER 8

Policy and Practice of LGBT Persons' Sport Participation in Colombia

Angélica María Sáenz-Macana, Javier Gil-Quintana, Sofía Pereira-García, and José Devís-Devís

INTRODUCTION

Sport is one of the most widespread leisure activities in the world and is considered a powerful socializing context into the cultural values of postindustrial societies (Coalter, 2007). However, as sport has been historically created by men and for men, it still maintains strong male socialization values (Kidd, 2013).

In fact, several authors consider that sport, more than any other social institution, perpetuates heteronormativity (Krane & Mann, 2014; Spaaij et al., 2015), which is 'the political, social, cultural and institutional power

A. M. Sáenz-Macana (✉) · J. Gil-Quintana
Faculty of Physical Activity and Sports Sciences, Universitat de València, Valencia, Spain
e-mail: anmasama@alumni.uv.es

S. Pereira-García · J. Devís-Devís
Faculty of Social Sciences, Universitat de València, Valencia, Spain

© The Author(s), under exclusive license to Springer Nature Switzerland AG 2021
J. Piedra and E. Anderson (eds.), *Lesbian, Gay, and Transgender Athletes in Latin America*, Palgrave Studies in Masculinity, Sport and Exercise, https://doi.org/10.1007/978-3-030-87375-2_8

and dominance of one or more groups, identities, behaviors, and/or practices over others' (Allen & Mendez, 2018, p. 74). This ideological system produces sex and gender inequalities, based on the idea of male superiority and female inferiority (Larsson, 2013).

Connell (1995) as well as Connell and Messerschmidt's (2005) revision of her work, call this name hegemonic masculinity. The idea here is that there is a social stratification, which generates discrimination, marginalization, and inequalities in the access, representation and athletic achievements of women and men with non-hegemonic masculinities in the realm of sport (English, 2017).

Moreover, the heteronormative contexts of sport often present less opportunities for LGBT (lesbian, gay, bisexual, and trans) persons' participation and reflects sexism, homonegativism, and transprejudice (Scandurra, et al., 2013; Symons et al., 2017). Several studies show the LGBT athletes are questioned for not fitting in heteronormative ideals and also face negative stereotypes, bigotry, and discrimination (Denison et al., 2021; Devís-Devís et al., 2017; Symons et al., 2017), although other studies show an increasing acceptance of homosexuality (Anderson et al., 2016; Bush et al., 2012; Magrath et al., 2015).

Within such contexts, many LGBT persons prefer to hide their gender and sexual identities to avoid being discriminated, judged, or negatively affected their sport career (Lawley, 2017; Moscowitz et al., 2019). It is, therefore, important to recognize the urgent need in creating an inclusive and safe sport environment to overcome barriers, prejudices, and stereotypes toward LGBT persons (Kulick et al., 2019).

However, more studies are necessary to enrich the existing knowledge on the conditions and experiences of LGBT people's participation in sport. Particular efforts are required from Latin-American countries where there is a lack of studies in the field of sport. This chapter thus provides a modest contribution to fill this gap by presenting what is known on policy and practice of LGBT persons' sport participation in Colombia.

THE POLICY CONTEXT IN COLOMBIA

According to the National Constitution of Colombia, freedom, dignity, and equal rights are granted to all Colombian citizens (Constitución Política de Colombia, 1991). This gives a legal pathway for LGBT people. In fact, between 1993 and 2016, the Constitutional Court issued more than 140 LGBT friendly rulings, all related to recognition their civil rights in several areas of social life: such as property, employment, health services, social security, same-sex marriage, adoption, and legal gender. These rights were developed in line with the Universal Declaration of Human Rights (United Nations, 2015) as a result of social, political, and legal struggles by local civil society organizations and grassroots activist movements (Albarracín, 2011; Corrales, 2015).

The most important legal document in force is the Anti-Discrimination Law, which in its Article 3 and 4 ruled against discrimination on grounds of race, nationality, sex, sexual orientation, religion, political ideology, or ethnic and cultural origin (Congreso de la República, 2011). This document places LGBT rights at the forefront of a Latin America movement in favor of this group of citizens (CDIH, 2018; Wilson & Gianella-Malca, 2019).

Despite this important legal advancement, however, the discrimination, assaults, and violence against members of the LGBT community are still commonplace in Colombia (CNMH, 2013; Lemaitre, 2009; Nagle, 2012; Promsex et al., 2020). For instance, there were 542 homicides in Colombia between January 2014 and June 2019, making Colombia the second highest in homicides of LGBT people in Latin America, behind Brazil (SInViolencia LGBTI, 2019). In addition, between 2007 and 2017, 44 social leaders of this community of people were assassinated in Colombia, and many others were victims of constant threats (CIDH, 2019). This scenario and the strong Christian influence, which has led to a counter-resistance movement against LGBT people impinged by Evangelic groups (Corrales & Sagarzazu, 2019; Lemaitre, 2013; López, 2018), suggest the necessity of ensuring the effective protection of LGBT rights to any social and cultural domain of Colombian life.

The sport domain was regulated by the Sport Law, number 181 from 1995, which established measures for the promotion of physical education and sport, recreation, and the use of leisure time in Colombia (Congreso de la República, 1995). This is an outdated law because it does not explicitly regulate issues regarding sexual or gender diversity, but stipulates the obligation of the State to guarantee the practice of sport, recreation and the use of free time of all people regardless their race, creed, condition, or sex.

Later policy documents added what was called a 'differential approach' for recognizing the rights of populations that traditionally and historically have been violated, marginalized, and discriminated (Ministerio del Interior, 2018). This approach reinforces the legal foundation for some public initiatives addressed to fulfill the rights of ethnic, gender, sexual, and cultural minorities in sport participation, such as the Bogotá policy guidelines for developing local sport activities with special reference the LGBT community (Alcaldía Mayor de Bogotá, 2017).

Recently, a protocol was approved for the prevention and eradication of gender-based violence in sports and physical activity (Ministerio del Deporte, 2020). This was a milestone policy document on gender issues in Colombian sport, because it stablished the legal conditions that legitimate the actions and programs for equitable and safe participation. However, the actual effective prevention of gender-based violence and equitable development of sport participation for minority groups is something yet to be realized, as cultural discrimination persists.

The Practice of LGBT Persons' Sport Participation in Colombia

Evidence-based knowledge is necessary in order to know the actual practice of LGBT participation in Colombian sport. However, there is no current review which facilitates this work in Colombia. For this reason, it is important to undertake a literature review to support how is developing the actual practice of LGBT sport participation in Colombia.

Initially, a search was conducted in the main international databases (WOS, Scopus, Sportdiscus, Pubmed, ERIC, and Dialnet), performed in November 2020 using the following combination of terms as search strategy: ((‘sexual diversity’ OR ‘gender diversity’ OR ‘LGBT’ OR lesbian OR gay OR bisexual OR transgender OR intersex) AND sport AND Colombia). The search was not limited to a particular period of time or any language. A single publication was found using these criteria, proving the scarcity of documents circulating through habitual international databases. This paper was about the lifestyle and LGBT people’s social practices in Bogotá that also includes sport practices (Barreto et al., 2010).

Due to the lack of papers obtained from the previous databases, the review also used grey literature for extending the search to other documents, thereby providing a more complete view of all available evidence (Mahood et al., 2014). The term grey literature is defined as publicly available, foreign or domestic, open-source information that is usually available in alternative channels or systems of publication, distribution, bibliographic control, or acquisition by book sellers or subscription agents (Benzies et al., 2006).

In particular, the grey literature search started by looking at the internet files of 24 physical education and sport research groups interested on gender issues and belonging to various Colombian universities. Most of their academic publications were focused on inequity issues among men/women and the female empowerment in sport context from different feminist perspectives. For instance, there were some documents about the situation of Colombian female soccer players, gender differences between male and women in physical activity, and girls and women's participation in sport (Hormiga, 2015; Lucumi, 2012; Martínez et al., 2019; Oxford & McLachlan, 2018).

A few other documents also referred to different discrimination and harassment situations experienced by non-heterosexual young people in schools (Colombia Diversa and Senttido, 2016; Kyu et al., 2020). However, although these documents focused on gender issues, most of these research groups were not interested in gender and sexual diversity related to physical education and sport. Only two documents were identified and specifically addressed to LGBT issues, since they raised several issues on transgender people's participation and the perception and beliefs on transgender people in physical education and sport (González, 2017, 2020).

The number of documents on LGBT issues was still short to gather substantial information and another search was conducted in the 9 sport newspapers with highest circulation in Colombia. From the 24 newspapers articles identified, only 5 presented substantial information to be added to the previous documents resulting in 8 documents the total that entered to the analysis (see Table 8.1). As a result of this analysis three broad categories emerged: sport participation, discrimination, and situations of support of LGBT people in Colombian sport.

Sport Participation

Colombian LGBTI participation in sport was well described in the cross-sectional survey based on a study developed by Barreto et al. (2010) with 343 LGBT and 296 heterosexual people from Bogotá. The aim was to identify the practices of consumption and lifestyle, including the sport and recreational activities of these participants. The results showed that there were differences in lifestyle between LGBT members and between

Table 8.1 Documents included in the analysis on the practice of LGBTI sport participation in Colombia

Authors (year)	Document type	Focus of interest	Methodology	Aim(s)
Barreto, Sandoval, and Cortes (2010)	Academic article	Consumer psychology, consumption, sport, LGBT	Survey	Identify the lifestyle (sporting and recreational activities) from LGBT and heterosexual people (Bogotá)
Redacción El País (17 Sep. 2016)	Newspaper article	Recreational Games, LGBT, sport, inclusion	News reporting	Report of the activities of the VII Recreational Games for LGBTI+ community (Cali)
EFE (16 May 2017)	Newspaper article	Sport, volleyball team, stereotypes, tournaments, transgender people	News reporting	Report of the experiences of trans-women in a women's volleyball team (Cundinamarca)
González (2017)	Degree dissertation	Beliefs, perceptions, transgender people, Physical Education and Sport	Mixed-method: • Autobiography • Questionnaire	Identify perceptions and beliefs toward transgender people in physical education and sport
Villa (16 Nov. 2017)	Newspaper article	LGBT, stereotypes, sport club, support	News reporting	Report of the experiences of an LGBT friendly sports club (Cali)
Lombana (20 Dec. 2018)	Newspaper article	Discrimination, lesbophobia, sport, female soccer	News reporting	Report on Camargo's discriminatory statements against women's football by sport manager, and politicians' reactions

(continued)

Table 8.1 (continued)

Authors (year)	Document type	Focus of interest	Methodology	Aim(s)
Marca Claro (29 Aug. 2019)	Newspaper article	Discrimination, lesbophobia, sport, female soccer, constitutional court	News reporting	Report the possible sanctions for Camargo's discriminatory statements against women's football
González (2020)	Academic article	Transgender people, gender identity, Physical Education and Sport	Theoretical Framework	Approaches to sexual diversity and physical education and sport: stereotypes and change initiatives

them and heterosexual people. However, these differences were specific and not attributable solely to sexual or gender identities.

The authors found that there were many more similarities than differences between women and gay men compared with their heterosexual counterparts, indicating that consumption was especially associated with demographic variables. The comparison of the subgroups of the LGBT population showed the following results:

- Higher percentages of lesbians, bisexual women, and gays play board games.
- Dance was mainly practiced by lesbians and bisexual women.
- Soccer was played by 21% of lesbians, 16.1% of bisexual women and 19.5% of bisexual men.
- Basketball was only practiced by lesbians' group.
- Volleyball was only practiced by bisexual men.
- Almost all the participants did aerobics or gym activities (19.7% of lesbians, 16.1% of bisexual women, 19.5% of bisexual men and 28.1% trans persons).
- Swimming was only practiced by bisexual women.
- Most trans persons and bisexual men preferred jogging or walking, activities also practiced by bisexual women and gays.
- Cycling was practiced by 16.1% of bisexual women and 20.9% of gays.

González's (2017) mixed-method study also mentioned the predilection a trans man showed by masculine activities in his childhood, such as soccer, as well as running, BMX freestyle and skateboard in his leisure time. Later, after his hormone treatment, he went to the gym mostly to increase his muscles and practiced other sports such as rugby and water polo.

In another study, González (2020) referred to a LGBT sports and recreational game events, developed in Cali and highlighted the low participation of athletes and fans in a recent edition probably because of the fear in their visibility and its undesirable consequences of violence and discrimination. Even so, several associations used sport as a strategy for the promotion of LGBT visibility in Colombia. This is the case of *Corporación Chaina*, which created a volleyball team of gay men in Cali to interact with the sport community and bring a message of respect.

The *GAPEF Gays futbolistas* in Bogotá also was created for making visible gay participation in soccer. Other examples of trans athletes' participation with media repercussion were Yanelle Zape Mendoza, a 100 m sprinter that competed in women's category to classify to Rio 2016 Olympic Games, and six other trans women who participated in the *Celta Femenino* volleyball club in Madrid-Cundinamarca (EFE, 16 May 2017; González, 2020).

Discrimination in Sport

The president of Tolima Club's statements about Colombian female soccer players represented a well-known case of LGBT discrimination in sport. He referred to them as heavy drinkers, 'more than men' and considered that their tournament was 'a breeding ground for lesbianism' (Lombana, 20 December 2018). This situation might generate lesbophobia, discriminatory expressions, and underestimation of female athletes' performances. Although the Anti-Discrimination Law was in force at the time, and stipulated sanctions, this act went unpunished by the civil and sporting institutions. This is because, according to the Colombian Soccer First Division, the apology was deemed sufficient (Marca Claro, 29 August 2019).

Other research-based documents report, discrimination, exclusion, marginalization, invisibility and, violence were experienced by trans persons in the sport context. For instance, the autobiography of a trans man in González's (2017) study showed he usually received insults, such as 'tomboy,' 'fag,' 'little girl,' or 'macho' in physical education and sport before his transition process. After his transition, he experienced exclusion, pressure, and discrimination in rugby and water polo sessions. Even at the university, in a sports class, he met a teacher who mocked homosexuals and lesbians. These experiences were in line with the perceptions of confusion, prejudice, and ignorance, as well as discriminatory opinions and negative evaluations that 30 students, physical education teachers, and coaches showed toward transgender people (González, 2017). Moreover, these perceptions fitted well with the traditional sports sex-segregation and the binary categorization of bodies and reflected that gender and sexual diversity are not recognized in the Colombian physical education and sport field (González, 2020).

Support in Sport

The analysis of the literature in this review also showed some positive perceptions on the need of providing facilities and safe spaces for the LGBT inclusion in the sport programs. It observed recognition that any citizen has the same rights to enjoy and gain benefits from physical education and sport. In fact, different initiatives developed at local and regional levels, especially in Bogotá, Medellín, and Cali, were committed to applying the policies presented in the previous section (González, 2017). Highlighted among them are some campaigns to promote sport participation among LGBT people (*Carrera de la visibilidad, Actívate por la igualdad, Juegos deportivos por la igualdad*) and the creation of a few LGBTI sport teams, especially in volleyball and soccer, which contributed to the visibility of these persons and their participation in sport events (EFE, 16 May 2017; Villa, 16 November 2017).

The city of Cali played a pioneering role in the recognition of gender and sexual diversity in sport, because, a few years ago, the Secretariat of Sports and Recreation and the Fundasfe Foundation hosted the Recreational Games for LGBT community. Among the planned activities were volleyball, soccer, swimming, jump rope, weightlifting, 5 K, and a high heel race. According to the organization, more than 500 persons participated in the events (Redacción El País, 17 September 2016), although it has not been developed its full potential resonance for gaining a wider visibility (González, 2020).

Another initiative of supporting LGBT participation in sport was the recent creation of the Commission for Gender Equity and Diversity by the Colombian Olympic Committee in 2020. This commission was in charge of promoting safe spaces in sport for women and LGBT people and protecting the athletes with gender and sexual diversity in high-level sporting competitions in Colombia.

FINAL COMMENTS

This chapter represents a first attempt to explore the policy and practice of LGBT people and sport participation in Colombia. It examined the types of sport LGBT people are engaged with, the discrimination and support experienced by them. It is obviously a modest contribution due to the limited attention it has received from rulers and policy makers, as well as the scarcity of data available to reconstruct the practice of LGBT sport participation. Further policy development, professional practices and studies are required in order to better understand how these persons achieve the same benefits than any other Colombian citizen: It a simple matter of social justice.

While the chapter presented limited knowledge around LGBT sport participation, it exudes important key issues to be considered in the near future. The first issue refers to the strengthening link between policy and practice by developing action plans with clear targets and verifiable schedules derived from the recent protocol for the prevention, care, and eradication of gender-based violence in sports and recreation (Ministerio del Deporte, 2020). We present several actions as examples:

- Carrying out awareness campaigns that make visible the sexual orientation and gender identity in sports fields and competitions, promoting anti-discrimination and eradicating LGBT phobia.
- Promoting education courses on LGBT issues and good practices for the staff of different physical education and sport organizations, such as governing bodies, federations, schools, clubs, facilities, teachers, and coaches' associations.
- Preventing, identifying, reporting, and addressing possible discriminations and violence cases through the Nacional Sport Observatory for improving safe and inclusive environments of practice.
- Strengthening the recent Commission for Gender Equity and Diversity of Colombian Olympic Committee.
- Increasing the participation of the LGBT people in physical activity and sport, and improving their physical, mental, and social wellbeing through special programs or by enriching the existing ones.

- Supporting the creation for LGBT sports clubs or teams to promote safe environments and to stimulate the inclusion of LGBT people in existing ones.

A second key issue concerns the widening gender perspective adopted by policy makers, sport managers, researchers, and people in general. The current perspective is reduced to gender issues and there is, therefore, an urgent need to adopt a diversity perspective around gender and sexual issues when developing policies and practices on sport participation.

We especially refer to the role researchers play in providing evidence-based knowledge as a third key issue. This is because academic work is important for evaluating and adjusting the policies and practices to finally facilitate access, participation, and positive experiences for LGBTI people. Therefore, it is necessary that researchers include other vulnerable groups on their research agendas for extending their gender interests beyond male/female issues, including LGBTI studies (Guerrero & Sutachan, 2012; Rodríguez & Ibarra, 2013).

Colombian researchers cannot continue ignoring the gender and sexual diversity in sport. Without clear information that reveals what is happening in schools, sport fields, gymnasiums, and other natural environments used for physical exercising, it would be difficult to make a clear diagnosis from which transform policies and practices for LGBT people, recognizing them as full citizens, as UNESCO has indicated (Kosciw & Pizmony-Levy, 2013).

It is important then to increase the production of research documents (theses, monographs, dissertations, and papers), especially articles that circulate by international databases on LGBTI studies from different theoretical perspectives (Castañeda et al., 2013; Cornejo et al., 2020). Moreover, this research production should be clearly committed to the eradication of all forms of discrimination, stigmatization, and violence derived from the extended heteronormativity in sport contexts.

Finally, in order to fulfill the previous three issues, it is important to promote a collaborative liaison among the different agents engaged in the policy and practice of LGBT sport participation in Colombia, mainly sport, LGBT and governing organizations, as well as universities, researchers, and professionals. The purpose of which is to build a network of allies that allows them to work in collaboration for linking policy and practice with evaluation until the LGBT sport participation in safe and inclusive environments becomes a reality.

References

Albarracín, M. (2011). Corte constitucional e movimentos sociais: O reconhecimento judicial dos direitos de casais do mesmo sexo na Colômbia. *SUR – Revista Internacional De Derechos Humanos, 8*(14), 7–33.

Alcaldía Mayor de Bogotá. (2017). *Línea Técnica Política Pública LGBTI. Sector cultura, recreación y deporte.* http://www.sdp.gov.co/sites/default/files/linea_cultura_pdf_0.pdf. Accessed 2 Nov 2020.

Allen, S., & Mendez, S. (2018). Hegemonic heteronormativity: Toward a new era of queer family theory. *Journal of Family Theory & Review, 10,* 70–86. https://doi.org/10.1111/jftr.12241

Anderson, E., Magrath, R., & Bullingham, R. (2016). *Out in sport: The experiences of openly gay men and lesbian in competitive sport.* Routledge.

Barreto, I., Sandoval, M., & Cortes, O. (2010). Prácticas de Consumo y estilo de vida de la población LGTB de Bogotá. *Revista Diversitas – Perspectivas En Psicología, 6*(1), 165–184.

Benzies, K. M., Premji, S., Hayden, K. A., & Serrett, K. (2006). State-of-the-evidence reviews: Advantages and challenges of including grey literature. *Worldviews on Evidence Based Nursing, 3,* 55–61. https://doi.org/10.1111/J.1741-6787.2006.00051.X

Bush, A., Anderson, E., & Carr, S. (2012). The declining existence of men's homophobia in British sport. *Journal for the Study of Sports and Athletes in Education, 6*(1), 107–120. https://doi.org/10.1179/ssa.2012.6.1.107

Castañeda, W., Pérez, A., Plata E., Cantiño, R., & Monsalve, D. (2013). *Voces y sentidos para re-pensar la diversidad sexual y de género en el Caribe colombiano.* https://caribeafirmativo.lgbt/docs/Voces%20&%20sentidos%20para%20re-pensar%20la%20diversidad%20sexual%20y%20de%20genero%20en%20el%20Caribe%20colombiano.pdf. Accessed 15 Oct 2020.

CDIH [Comisión Interamericana de Derechos Humanos]. (2018). *Avances y Desafíos hacia el reconocimiento de los derechos de las personas LGBTI en las Américas.* http://www.oas.org/es/cidh/informes/pdfs/LGBTI-ReconocimientoDerechos2019.pdf. Accessed 5 Oct 2020.

CDIH [Comisión Interamericana de Derechos Humanos]. (2019). *Informe sobre la situación de personas defensoras de derechos humanos y líderes sociales en Colombia.* http://www.oas.org/es/cidh/informes/pdfs/DefensoresColombia.pdf. Accessed 5 Oct 2020.

CNMH [Centro Nacional de Memoria Histórica]. (2013). *BASTA YA! Colombia: Memorias de guerra y dignidad.* Imprenta Nacional.

Coalter, F. (2007). *A wider social role for Sport. Who's keeping the score?* Routledge.

Colombia Diversa and Sentiido. (2016). Encuesta de Clima Escolar LGBT en Colombia. Mi Voz Cuenta. *Experiencias de Adolescentes y Jóvenes Lesbianas, Gays, Bisexuales y Trans en el ámbito escolar.* https://colombiadiversa.org/publicaciones/voz-cuenta-encuesta-clima-escolar-lgbt-colombia-2016. Accessed 7 May 2020.

Congreso de la Republica. (1995). *Ley 181 de 1995*. https://www.mindep orte.gov.co/recursos_user/2019/Juridica/Normograma/Leyes/Ley-181-de-1995.pdf. Accessed 14 Oct 2020.

Congreso de la Republica. (2011). *Ley 1482 de 2011*. http://www.secretari asenado.gov.co/senado/basedoc/ley_1482_2011.html#:~:text=El%20nuevo%20texto%20es%20el,y%20dem%C3%A1s%20razones%20de%20discriminaci%C3%B3n.&text=Actos%20de%20Racismo%20o%20discriminaci%C3%B3n. Accessed 14 Oct 2020.

Connell, R. (1995). *Masculinities*. University of California Press.

Connell, R., & Messerschmidt, J. (2005). Hegemonic masculinity: Rethinking the concept. *Gender and Society, 19*(6), 829–859. https://doi.org/10.1177/0891243205278639

Constitución Política de Colombia [Const.] (1991). Editorial Leyer.

Cornejo, G., Martínez, J., & Vidal-Ortiz, S. (2020). LGBT studies without LGBT studies: Mapping alternative pathways in Perú and Colombia. *Journal of Homosexuality, 67*(3), 417–434. https://doi.org/10.1080/00918369.2018.1534411

Corrales, J. (2015). *LGBT rights and representation in Latin America and the Caribbean: The influence of structure, movements, institutions, and culture.* University of North Carolina.

Corrales, J., & Sagarzazu, I. (2019). Not all "Sins" are rejected equally: Resistance to LGBT rights across religions in Colombia. *Politics and Religion, 13*(2), 351–377.

Denison, E., Bevan, N., & Jeanes, R. (2021). Reviewing evidence of LGBTQ+ discrimination and exclusion in sport. *Sport Management Review, 24*(3), 389–409. https://doi.org/10.1016/j.smr.2020.09.003

Devís-Devís, J., Pereira-Garcia, S., Valencia-Peris, A., Fuentes-Miguel, J., López-Cañada, E., & Pérez-Samaniego, V. (2017). Harassment patterns and risk profile in Spanish trans persons. *Journal of Homosexuality, 64*(2), 239–255. https://doi.org/10.1080/00918369.2016.1179027

EFE (2017, May 16). Equipo de transexuales quiere un espacio en el voleibol colombiano. *El Tiempo*. https://www.eltiempo.com/deportes/otros-dep ortes/equipo-de-transexuales-quiere-un-espacio-en-el-voleibol-colombiano-88728. Accessed 6 Dec 2020.

English, C. (2017). Toward sport reform: Hegemonic masculinity and reconceptualizing competition. *Journal of the Philosophy of Sport, 44*(2), 183–198. https://doi.org/10.1080/00948705.2017.1300538

González, J. (2017). *Creencias y Percepciones sobre el cuerpo y la identidad de las personas transgénero en el campo de la educación física y el deporte en la ciudad de Cali.* (Trabajo de Grado). Universidad del Valle. https://bibliotecadigital. univalle.edu.co/bitstream/handle/10893/13525/3484-0525661.pdf;jsessi onid=5714EE3571BFC271CC034B6E0C0D5B29?sequence=1. Accessed 27 Sep 2020.

González, J. (2020). Educación Física y Deporte Trans-formado. *Praxis, Educación y Pedagogía, 4*, 78–97. https://doi.org/10.25100/praxis_educac ion.v0i4.9121

Guerrero, O., & Sutachan, H. (2012). "En Colombia se puede ser...": Indagaciones sobre la producción de lo LGBT desde la Academia ["in Colombia you can be..." academic inquires on the LGTB production]. *Nómadas, 37*, 219–229.

Hormiga, C. (2015). Perspectiva de género en el estudio de la práctica de actividad física. *Revista Ciencias De La Salud, 13*(2), 233–248. https://doi. org/10.1080/17430437.2013.785757

Kidd, B. (2013). Sports and masculinity. *Sport in Society, 16*(4), 553–564.

Kosciw, J., & Pizmony-Levy, O. (2013). International perspectives on homophobic and transphobic bullying in schools. *Journal of LGBT Youth, 13*(1–2), 1–5. https://doi.org/10.1080/19361653.2015.1101730

Krane, V., & Mann, M. (2014). Heterosexism, homonegativism, and transprejudice. In R. Eklund & G. Tenenbaum (Eds.), *Encyclopedia of sport and exercise psychology* (pp. 336–338). SAGE.

Kulick, A., Wernick, L., Espinoza, M., Newman, T., & Desselet, A. (2019). Three strikes and you're out: Culture, facilities, and participation among LGBTQ youth in sports. *Sport, Education and Society, 24*(9), 939–953. https://doi.org/10.1080/13573322.2018.1532406

Kyu, S., Divsalar, S., Flórez-Donado, J., Kittle, K., Lin, A., Meyer, I., & Torres-Salazar, P. (2020). *Stress, Health, and Wellbeing of LGBT People in Colombia Results from a National Survey*. School of Law Williams Institute. https://williamsinstitute.law.ucla.edu/publications/lgbt-people-col ombia/. Accessed 7 May 2020.

Larsson, H. (2013). Sport physiology research and governing gender in sport – A power–knowledge relation? *Sport, Education and Society, 18*(3), 334–348. https://doi.org/10.1080/13573322.2011.582095

Lawley, S. (2017). LGBT+ participation in sports: 'Invisible' participants, 'Hidden' spaces of exclusion. In V. Caven & S. Nachmias (Eds.), *Hidden Inequalities in the Workplace* (pp. 155–179). Palgrave Macmillan.

Lemaitre, J. (2009). El amor en tiempos de cólera: Derechos LGBT en Colombia. *SUR – Revista Internacional de Derechos Humanos, 6*(11), 79–97.

Lemaitre, J. (2013). *Laicidad y resistencia: movilización católica contra los derechos sexuales y reproductivos en América Latina*. Instituto de Investigaciones Jurídicas-Universidad Nacional Autónoma de México.

Lombana, C. (20 december 2018). El mundo reclama por las declaraciones de Gabriel Camargo sobre el fútbol femenino. *Diario online marca*. https://co. marca.com/claro/futbol/liga/2020/12/28/5fe91ab1268e3eb4498b45cf. html. Accessed 6 Dec 2020.

López, J. (2018). Movilización y contramovilización frente a los derechos lGBTI. Respuestas conservadoras al reconocimiento de los derechos humanos. *Estudios Sociológicos, 36*(106), 161–187. https://doi.org/10.24201/es.2018v3 6n106.1576

Lucumi, Y. (2012). Aportes de la mujer en la transformación de los estereotipos socio-culturales del deporte colombiano [Women contributions to the transformation of the sociocultural stereotypes of Colombian sport]. *Revista U.D.C.A Actualidad & Divulgación Científica, 15,* 27–35.

Magrath, R., Anderson, E., & Roberts, S. (2015). "On the door-step of equality: Attitudes toward gay athletes among academy-level footballers. *International Review for the Sociology of Sport, 50*(7), 804–821. https://doi.org/10.1177/1012690213495747

Mahood, Q., Van Eerd, D., & Irvin, E. (2014). Searching for grey literature for systematic reviews: Challenges and benefits. *Research Synthesis Methods, 5*(3), 221–234. https://doi.org/10.1002/jrsm.1106

Marca Claro. (29 August 2019). Corte Constitucional pide a Dimayor y Federación rendir cuentas por el 'tema Camargo'. *Diario online marca.* https://co.marca.com/claro/futbol/liga/2019/08/29/5d683e282 68e3e73588b456e.html. Accessed 6 Dec 2020.

Martínez, C., Goellner, S., & Orozco, A. (2019). Fútbol y mujeres: El panorama de la Liga Profesional Femenina de Fútbol de Colombia. *Educación Física y Deporte, 38*(1). https://doi.org/10.17533/udea.efyd.v38n1a03

Ministerio del Deporte (2020). *Protocolo para la prevención, atención y erradicación de las violencias basadas en género en el deporte, la recreación, la actividad física y el aprovechamiento del tiempo libre.* https://www.mindep orte.gov.co/recursos_user/2020/viceministerio/Protocolo_para_la_prevenc ion_atencion_y_erradicacion_de_las_violencias_basadas_en_genero_en_el_dep orte.pdf. Accessed 2 Nov 2020.

Ministerio del Interior. (2018). *Decree 762 of 2018. Política Pública para la garantía del ejercicio efectivo de los derechos de las personas que hacen parte de los sectores sociales LGBTI y de personas con orientación sexual e identidad de género diversas.* https://www.mininterior.gov.co/la-institucion/normativi dad/decreto-762-del-7-de-mayo-de-2018-politica-publica-garantia-de-los-der echos-sectores-sociales-lgbti. Accessed 2 Nov 2020.

Moscowitz, L., Billings, A., Ejaz, K., & O'Boyle, J. (2019). Outside the sports closet: New discourses of professional gay male athletes in the mainstream. *Journal of Communication Inquiry, 43*(3), 249–271. https://doi.org/10.1177/0196859918808333

Nagle, L. (2012). Giving shelter from the storm: Colombians fleeing persecution based on sexual orientation. *Tulsa Law Review, 48*(1), 1–26.

Oxford, S., & McLachlan, F. (2018). "You Have to Play Like a Man, But Still be a Woman": Young female Colombians negotiating gender through participation in a Sport for Development and Peace (SDP) organization. *Sociology of Sport Journal, 35*(3), 258–267. https://doi.org/10.1123/ssj.2017-0088

Promsex, Colombia Diversa and Cattrachas. (2020). *Informe Trinacional: litigio estratégico de casos de violencia por prejuicio por orientación sexual, identidad y expresión de género en Colombia, Perú y Honduras*, https://colombiadiversa. org/colombiadiversa2016/wp-content/uploads/2020/05/INF-TRINAC IONAL_PRSX_FINAL-BKUP.pdf. Accessed 2 Nov 2020.

Redacción El País. (17 September 2016). Este domingo arrancan los Juegos Lgbti, *Periódico diario El País*, https://www.elpais.com.co/deportes/este-domingo-arrancan-los-juegos-lgbti.html. Accessed 6 Dec 2020.

Rodríguez, A., & Ibarra, M. (2013). Los estudios de género en Colombia. Una discusión preliminar [Gender Studies in Colombia. A Preliminary Discussion]. *Sociedad y Economía, 24*, 15–46.

Scandurra, C., Picariello, S., Amodeo, A., & Valerio, P. (2013). Heteronormativity, homophobia and transphobia in sport. In Interuniversity Centre for Bioethics Research (Eds.), *Bioethical issues by the Interuniversity Center for Bioethics Research (C.I.R.B.)* (pp. 195–211). Editoriale Scientifica.

SInViolencia LGBTI (2019). *El prejuicio no conoce fronteras: Homicidios de lesbianas, gay, bisexuales, trans e intersex en países de América Latina y el Caribe 2014 – 2019*. Alta Voz Editores, https://sinviolencia.lgbt/wp-content/uploads/2019/08/Informe_Prejuicios_compressed.pdf. Accessed 28 Oct 2020.

Spaaij, R., Farquharson, K., & Marjoribanks, T. (2015). Sport and social Inequalities. *Sociology Compass, 9*(5), 400–411. https://doi.org/10.1111/soc4.12254

Symons, C., O'Sullivan, G. A., & Polman, R. (2017). The impacts of discriminatory experiences on lesbian, gay and bisexual people in sport. *Annals of Leisure Research, 20*(4), 467–489. https://doi.org/10.1080/11745398. 2016.1251327

United Nations. (2015) *Universal Declaration of Human Rights*. https://www.un.org/en/udhrbook/pdf/udhr_booklet_en_web.pdf. Accessed 8 Oct 2020.

Villa, C. (2017, November 16). Experiencias junto a los "otros", los LGBT. *Las 2orillas*. https://www.las2orillas.co/experiencias-junto-los-otros-los-lgbt. Accessed 6 Dec 2020.

Wilson, B., & Gianella-Malca, C. (2019). Overcoming the limits of legal opportunity structures: LGBT Rights' divergent paths in Costa Rica and Colombia. *Latin American Politics and Society, 61*(2), 138–163. https://doi.org/10. 1017/lap.2018.76

PART III

Transgender Issues and Sports

CHAPTER 9

Trans Masculinities on the Sport Courts of Brazil, "The Country of Football"

Julian Pegoraro Silvestrin and Alexandre Fernández-Vaz

In this chapter,[1] we introduce the emergence of trans masculine football teams in Brazil. Football is part of the invention of Brazilian national identity, and, as such, builds expectations about bodies as well as rejections of others. From the visibility of these teams, we discuss the negotiations of masculinity performances and sociability and competitiveness issues. We accomplish this through field research with participant observation during the year of 2019 and early 2020, in São Paulo, where there are three teams of trans masculine *futsal*[2] players. We also conducted interviews with four *futsal* players[3] and examined articles published online in newspapers and sport blogs about the teams and the competitions they participate in.

Since the 1990s, meetings have been held in Brazil to create associations of *travestis*[4] and trans women, aiming to establish a network of political organization. Trans masculinities, however, only began to promote meetings and start to organize themselves in associations at the

J. P. Silvestrin (✉) · A. Fernández-Vaz
Federal University of Santa Catarina (UFSC), Florianópolis, Brazil

J. Piedra and E. Anderson (eds.), *Lesbian, Gay, and Transgender Athletes in Latin America*, Palgrave Studies in Masculinity, Sport and Exercise, https://doi.org/10.1007/978-3-030-87375-2_9

end of the first decade of the 2000s. Together, these organizations have fought primarily for legal equality. While this chapter is about sport, a short discussion provides context.

The journey for recognition and rights is long, but since 2018, we have had Social Name Policy, a governmental strategy that guarantees the use of the first name with which the individual recognizes himself, and not registered at birth, in different spheres of society, such as education and work. Regarding the change of the first name in the official identification documents, since 2018, this can be done without the need to open a legal process.

Brazil is at an interesting intersection of liberalization for trans issues, alongside neoconservative politics. This means that we have gained some formal recognition through laws around protection and name changing, but there is also a great deal of social hostility from those opposed. This combination means that there are lots of trans organizations, but that also Brazil has the highest rate of trans women murders in the world[5] (Benevides & Nogueira, 2021).

In Brazil we don't have specific policies among trans athletes, and in some cases, the norms of the International Olympic Committee are followed. But further evidencing the influence of neoconservatives, several bills have been drafted that aim to forbid the participation of trans people in sports competitions in the gender category according to self-identification, by claiming that the anatomical sexual difference must define the category which body belongs to.

Although we have few trans athletes working at a high-performance level in Brazil, there is an expressive movement of trans masculinities grouping around the sports practice. More intensely, around the descending modalities of football, which is a sport that carries throughout the twentieth century in Brazil a narrative of national and masculine identity.

We understand trans masculinities as expressions and gender identifications that come from individuals who were biopolitically assigned as female at birth, but who recognize their existence in male corporeality (Repolês, 2017), transitioning each one in his own way. The term encompasses different nominations, trans men, non-binary, among other identifications that do not necessarily claim the category man. Likewise, we use the term cisgender (cis) as a category that demarcates the constructed and artificial character of the gender identity of those people in accordance with the gender attributed to their birth.

Trans masculinities in football in Brazil appear at the same time that "homosexualities" are organizing themselves in associations and building championships. It is in this movement that the initial performances of "Meninos Bons de Bola" (MBB), the first trans masculine *futsal* association formed in 2016 in the largest city in the country, São Paulo.

They are minor teams of *futsal* and 7-a-side football,[6] but end up playing matches in several modalities that descend from football according to the events they participate in, such as friendly matches, festivals and tournaments geared to sexual and gender diversity. Some of these teams aim to be part of the amateur competitive circuit and, in common, appear as a proposal for trans-male engagement in a sports activity, in addition to a socialization space based on identity recognition.

THE TEAMS

MBB arises in 2016 from the initiative of a trans man who worked at the Reference Center in Defense of Diversity (a space for welcoming and assisting LGBT people in São Paulo) together with a local psychologist. Both realized that trans men did not access the center's actions as much as the other individuals of the acronym LGBT and decided to make a call via social networks (publicizing the activity in WhatsApp groups and Facebook pages) for a conversation circle for trans men followed by a football match. Approximately thirty men attended, and it was decided to repeat the meeting frequently, which happened, to the point of forming a team.

Initially they trained in a public park, but they have left the local under threats and transphobic injuries from the other users and moved to a private court offered by a trade union. This fact leads us to Arendt, which affirms that plurality is what characterizes the human condition. It means, the plurality implies to recognize that difference makes us unique. This singularity in difference is what qualifies us for political participation (Arendt, 2010).

In this case, although migrating to a private court allows better training conditions, we should pay attention for the restriction of a citizen right, to take part in a public place. The expulsion of trans bodies from public space denunciate a mark the denial of the condition of citizens of these bodies. Citizenship and, therefore, access to the city still presuppose a cisgender body (Silvestrin & Fernandez-Vaz, 2020).

In 2019, other exclusively trans masculine teams were formed, seeking sociability around the practice of sports. Among them was BigTBoys, a society football team from the city of Rio de Janeiro founded also by a trans man who is a local activist, and two more *futsal* teams from the city of São Paulo: Transversão FC and Os T Mosqueteiros. These last two train together in the format of workshops offered on the court of "Casa Florescer" (Special Reception Center for Transsexual Women), an institution that houses trans women and transvestites in situation of social vulnerability. The creator of Transversão states that, "football is the sport of the Brazilian and it is through it that I was able to access trans boys." There is, therefore, a narrow relationship between LGBT activism and the formation of these teams.

Even though the Southeast is the Brazilian region with the most trans masculine teams and organizations, we can see the emergence of teams in other parts of the country. In 2018 Transviver F.C. was born, in the city of Recife. The team is part of the non-governmental organization Instituto Transviver which aims to provide psychosocial support to the LGBT community with a focus on trans people. Transviver's activities began with informal games among its members, the so-called *pelada*, and later a trainer was integrated into the group, however, the team never competed.

The trans teams mentioned train only once a week on Sundays. It means that the only moment they have to dedicate to the practice is on time off the duties, at a leisure time, not as a major competitive intention. The sessions are sometimes guided by trans men who are physical education students, sometimes by the most experienced players of the team. However, women who also have experience in football often take on that task voluntarily, but they do not remain with the teams for a sufficient period to carry out more consistent technical work.

The turnover of players who pass through the teams is also high. It is common for the same person to be part of a team, sometimes another, and rarely do players know what their playing position is. We can attribute this to the diversity of sporting experiences and skills (from ex-players in the youth system categories of professional football or other sports to people who have never participated in training sessions) and with different goals (leisure, meeting with other trans people, participate in competitions).

Other factors influence the performance of these teams. They are composed of a diversity of bodies that are in different moments of transition and that use different technologies of masculinization of bodies. Hormone bodies with synthetic testosterone along with others that do not use this substance, with surgery to remove the breasts or pectorals compressed by binders disguise the breasts, fat, withered or strong due to muscle hypertrophy exercises.

These diversities create different rhythms for the team itself, bringing, with the support of other ones, the power of resistance and visibility, but also facing an impasse in the face of the desire and demand for sporting competitiveness. Some of the best players have high performance and look for competitive experiences, while others have no sports background, finding big difficulties with elementary techniques.

In addition to the participation of championships with greater competitive appeal, which we will address below, we highlight the friendly matches. In friendly and festivals matches, teams play against other ones of different compositions: male, gay, female, lesbian, mixed (with male and female players, trans and cis), and inclusive (which bring together the most varied sexual and gender identities).

Following these trans masculine teams we realized that as a tool for trans masculine subjectivation, sport becomes a space for the construction of oneself, for the elaboration of new forms of life based on the identification and recognition of the bodies present at the practice arena. One of our participants who was responsible for creating a trans masculine team said:

> When there is an invitation [to play] it is from cis gay male team and we go as invited participants and the competition is not the main objective, the important thing is to occupy the place, interact and socialize with others. (interview of 12 February, 2020)

These trans teams are spaces for sociability and socialization, where rules, codes, values of masculinity and sport are transmitted. But, it is also a space to questioning this same masculinities and sport valued attributes to masculinity, like aggressiveness, something uncommon in male milieus (Connell, 1995). We will come back to this topic later, but the following excerpt shows the tension caused by a way of playing that demands the body to be power and strength:

We are like "oh, the guy is rough!", "oh, all the time he comes roughly and hurts me!". I say "fuck, so stop playing ball, sit in the bleachers and watch it because it's contact". (interview of 10 December, 2019)

The speech demonstrates the importance of continuing to play even if the game gets tough because of some physical contact during the match, because masculinity is thought to be aggressive.

THE COMPETITIONS

Trans masculinities in sport reach a new level when competitions are organized. In June 2017, the first edition of the São Paulo Diversity Games took place, organized by the LGBT Sports Committee (CDG-Brazil) and the São Paulo LGBT Pride Association (APOGLBT) during Diversity Week, as part of the official LGBT Pride Parade program. The Games that year had four associations, three of which consisted of gay cisgender men and one of trans men (MBB) in the *futsal* modality. MBB won a game in the penalty shootout against a newly formed seven-a-side football team. In the dispute for third place, despite being defeated by dozens of goals, MBB ends with the bronze medal. This was because, throughout the championship, its athletes suffered transphobia from an apparently not warned team about trans masculinities that claimed the MBB players were women and not men. The posture of the team that delegitimized the gender identity of these players was pointed out to the organization, which then decided to disqualify the team in question.

Different from the Global North where lesbian and gay sports organizations and leagues somehow have been around since the 1970s (Symons, 2004; Travers, 2006), in Brazil, it is only in 2017 that an organized league takes part, when the LiGay Nacional de Futebol and Champions LiGay—an amateur league inspired by the format of the British Gay Football Supporters Network—GFSN National League and society football—were founded. Other competitions also took place that year, such as the Hornet Football Cup of Diversity, in São Paulo (which bears the name and brand of a relationship app aimed at the gay public), and the Champions Alliance, in Curitiba, capital of a state the southern region of the country. This last event had the participation of MBB. According to one of our interlocutors, the performance of the team was inferior to those cis teams and the audience (mostly LGBT people) responded by sexist and transphobic jokes.

In the same year, the association celebrated its first anniversary during the "Ocupa Pacaembu Festival," an event organized by the Football Museum in partnership with collectives of artists, activists, and football teams from the peripheries. It took place at Charles Miller Square, in front of the Pacaembu Stadium, in São Paulo, and at the time a player stated: "I am happy here today because my body can exist in this place."[7] Resuming the experiences of delegitimity in gay championships and the expulsion from the public court, this statement alerts us that if a body can exist there, in other places it cannot. This is serious, since the right to life and a dignified existence is formally guaranteed to Brazilian citizens. A dignified life comes from relationships in the public space and presupposes the recognition of differences and coexistence (Silvestrin & Fernandez-Vaz, 2020).

In 2018, there was another tension involving the participation of MBB in the championship. It was a weekend that the MBB conceded 40 goals in six games and scored only 1. The championship was the second Hornet Football Cup of Diversity, which in a year went from eight participating teams to 15. This represents the growth of football aimed at the LGBT audience in Brazil. One interlocutor tells of tough games, in which the team was not at the same technical level as their opponents. Opponents from the second game onwards realized that the MBB was a team to be defeated with a large number of goals, which would contribute to a better placement in the championship if the dispute was decided on goal difference. During that game the referee told the trans players that the most skillful among them was precisely the cis man.

In the last two games of the championship the team was authorized by the opponents to play with one more athlete. The central referee, upset, was slow to authorize, addressing female players. Both opponents and referees, according to an interlocutor, were not in the least prepared to deal with the diversity highlighted in the name of the competition. They heard statements like: "If they don't beat these girls, this team can stop, right, guys?" and "they want to play with men, but they are only women playing."

Such situations reveal the misogyny and transphobia present in sports even if practiced by non-heterosexual individuals. That shows "sport has a special place in society for reinforcing these standard versions of sex, gender and sexuality" (Symons, 2004, p. 411). So the cisnormativity of the practice lies in the supposed linearity between sex and gender as a norm: trans men are seen as women and therefore play badly.

The relevance of the adjective diversity linked to these championships is also questioned, after all, the predominance is of associations and male, white, cisgender, gay and well-trained bodies (Camargo, 2020). A fact that also raised doubts for the trans team to the point of questioning the legitimacy and desire to be there, after all, in addition to not being at a similar level of performance, most trans men who make up these teams identify themselves as heterosexual.

We believe that event organizations that intend to be inclusive of diversities should create strategies aiming to avoid these comments inside the court and outside, or even coming from the fans. It is possible to gather with referees and players before matches to discuss these issues, or to include clauses in the regulations that punish prejudiced attitudes, and also warn the audience.

The first match between trans associations in Rio de Janeiro took place in 2019. In a friendly match, Meninos Bons de Bola and BigT-Boys faced each other, in the society football modality. In the same year, teams from São Paulo faced each other on two occasions: at the "Trans-Esportes" event, organized by Casa Florescer, with the aim of bringing together the trans community in inclusive bodily practices and political-cultural debates, and at the MBB third Anniversary Festival. At its festival, MBB was disqualified after losing the first match against a team of lesbian women. Transversão was also disqualified after losing its first game to Os T Mosqueteiros, the only trans masculine team that goes a little further in the competition.

These individuals affirm that the reception of trans boys in sport and their visibility are more important and assume that to compete it is necessary to have technical training and financial resources, elements that the teams do not have. But even in friendly disputes, it is often heard that they "can no longer bear to be beaten." We understand that without systematic and minimally oriented work toward the game and disputes, there is not much room for positive gaming experiences to emerge. Although there are skilled players, the teams are far from any competitive level. Its importance still lies in the encounter and visibility of their bodies, in the possibility of being able to play football again for some and in the opportunity, for others, to experience it.

Sports and Masculinities

Although we have been discussing the relationship between sport and masculinities throughout the chapter, it is worth remembering that the attributes on which sport rises are mainly those incorporated by boys and men as a symbol of virility and masculinity: competition, violence, combat, dominance over their bodies and other men and women (Messner, 1989). Current works like Anderson (2014) recognize that the relationship between sport and masculinity has shifted substantially and show that sports are no longer a bastion of homophobia and sexism, especially in the Global North/West. But this is not the reality of Global South in general, particularly is not the Brazilian reality as we demonstrate throughout this chapter.

The existence of specific competitions for LGBT athletes, therefore, does not guarantee that the specificities and diversity of gender identity will be understood and respected. These leagues allow major variety of gender expressions but still is binary, sport it is not a welcoming space for trans people (Travers, 2006). Although Traver's diagnose has fifteen years, this is still the case of Brazil. One of the reasons for increased hostility to trans people, compared to sexual minorities, is that sport is predicated on a sex-binary. Thus, in Camargo (2012) ethnography of the Gay Games and other LGBT games, from 2008 to 2011, they show that trans people were on the sidelines in these competitions, pointing out the difficulty of including them in the gender categories by their self-identification and access to bathrooms and changing rooms, for example.

Exclusive competitions also do not suggest that these athletes restrict themselves to them, but they are an additional possibility for those who have already been excluded or feel they have no place in the standardized sport because of their sexuality or gender identity.

Another scene that reflects the constant negotiation between the desire for the practice and the identity statement is in the story of a Transviver player:

> We were invited to a friendly match that was a friendly one for the opening of a championship only for lesbian women. And it was an opening, right? It was just an opening, introducing the team... we should be presented as a team of trans men and such, some people agreed for the visibility, the importance, and others not because they were still afraid to get there and suffer prejudice and such. But I believe it would have been an interesting experience too. (interview of 16 October, 2020)

The refusal to play at a women's event tells us of the refusal to return to occupy a place from which they have already left, after all, they are constantly struggling for the recognition of their belonging to the male sports category, as well as that of men. It is important to highlight that in geopolitical terms, Transviver is based in a capital of the northeast region of Brazil and the others in what we named the South-Southeast hub, for historical reasons, holds the country's economic and cultural hegemony. The location makes it easier for associations to meet and create leagues and championships. This is not the reality of Transviver, isolated from these competitions.

In addition to the situations presented above, which show the tension and the negotiation of sporting and gender performances, it was witnessed on the field that in moments of more forceful plays, in which the "body game" prevails, are seen as aggressive, as perpetuation of a toxic masculinity. Displeased, one of the players, also a trans masculine person, pointed out that they were all very sensitive and added: "Aren't you a man? Then kick like a man! Be a man!" (Field note from 4 November 2019). This kind of comment reinforces, at least in Brazil, what Travers (2006, p. 432) wrote: "sport teaches and reinforces a key social lesson: it is not only better to be a boy than a girl, but it is also a matter of social survival for boys to prove that they are not anything like girls and therefore not gay."

Football played by trans masculine people (mostly self-styled trans men) is a space where, on the one hand, the expressions of a hegemonic masculinity are disputed, but on the other, masculinities are also regulated by measuring the *quantum* of virility is present in the other. There is a contradiction between its disruptive potential and the reiteration of the norm, because, as we saw earlier, the masculinity dimension of sport is what makes the rejection of everything that is considered feminine and, therefore, next to women and gays.

FINAL CONSIDERATIONS

In recent years, with the social recognition of gender identities beyond the medical-legal instances, more people have been able to name themselves trans and, while trans, a greater number of individuals have been able to access the most varied social spaces, sport is one of them. This is another space for the identification and construction of trans masculinities.

On the other hand, tans masculinities tension the normative structures on which sport is founded (in binary categories that end up justifying the level of performance expected for each body) and are, at the same time, questioned in the manifestations that reiterate the norm. We perceive a constant negotiation between gender and sports performances by the individuals involved in the practice.

The presence of trans teams is very recent in the history of Brazilian football. Seen as political collectives, although not all the individuals that compose these associations understand them as such, they are called to the public by sports event organizers, LGBT activists, and also by the media, for political participation. However, the questions that these bodies provoke are not always well received, generating tensions and making visible, also in sports, the precariousness of these bodies when exposed to the other.

The appearance of these bodies in the public space playing sports, and especially football, adds a weight to the questioning of a monolithic identity linked to the land of football that has been thinking about the multiplicity of football played here. We hope that the situations narrated throughout these pages can contribute to the formulation of other ways of conceiving and playing sports, in which each practitioner can, in his own way, even in accordance with the established rules, enjoy the game and his body.

NOTES

1. This is an excerpt from a doctoral research in progress, and some considerations presented here were previously discussed in two other works, from whose it retakes (literally or not) some fragments: Silvestrin, J. P. and Fernandez-Vaz, A. (2020). *Meninos Bons de Bola: transmasculinidades em quadra*. CSOnline (31), pp.158–167; Silvestrin, J. P. and Fernandez-Vaz, A. (2021). *Transmasculinidades no esporte: entre corpos e práticas dissonantes*, Revista Estudos Feministas, Volume 29 (2), pp.1–13.

2. *Futsal* is how the 5-a-side football is known in Brazil. This is a very popular modality of football in the country, and it is played on a hard surface court, with five players on each team and no limits for substitution. A match lasts for 40 minutes divided into two 20 minute of play ball.

3. We interviewed four *futsal* players. Respecting the self-identification, two heterosexual trans men aged 25 and 28 years old who in terms of race declared themselves as *pardo* (a nomination of color from the miscegenation in Brazil) and they are University students; a 31-year-old white trans masculine who is science teacher and a 44-year-old black trans man who is historian and multi-artist. Only the oldest of them has played professional football in the youth division.

4. *Travesti* is a recognized Brazilian political-identity category. Raewyn Connell [in Connell, R. (2016) *Gênero em termos reais*. Translated by Mosckovich, M. São Paulo: nVersos] pays attention to the friction that the expansion of the notion of transsexuality—starting from hegemonic categories, theories and ways of life in the Global North—causes in local experiences. In Brazil, the imported image of the transgender woman is closer to an ideal of whiteness of femininity and in shock with the aesthetics and corporeality of the *travesti* that is often associated with racialized and precarious street prostitution.

5. According to the dossier of assassinate and violence against trans people in Brazil, formulated annually by the non-governmental organizations ANTRA (National Association of *Travestis* and Transsexuals) and IBTE (Brazilian Institute of Trans Education). This document is available at: https://antrabrasil.files.wordpress.com/2021/01/dossie-trans-2021-29jan2021.pdf [Accessed 24 March 2021].

6. 7 a side football is a modality played by seven players on each team and no limits for substitution. The playing field has synthetic grass and is reduced in size compared to traditional football and the match lasts 50 minutes divided into two 25 minutes of play ball.

7. Camargo, W. X. (2017). Ocupa Pacaembu: futebol de rua, arte, vivências. *Ludopédio*, 99(3) Available at: https://www.ludopedio.com.br/arquibancada/ocupa-pacaembu/ [Accessed 24 March 2021].

References

Anderson, E. (2014). *21st century jocks: Sporting men and contemporary hetero-sexuality.* Palgrave Macmillan.

Arendt, H. (2010). *A condição humana.* Forense Universitária.

Benevides, B., & Nogueira, S. (Eds.). (2021). *Dossiê dos assassinatos e da violência contra travestis e transexuais brasileiras em 2020.* Expressão Popular, ANTRA, IBTE. https://antrabrasil.files.wordpress.com/2021/01/dossie-trans-2021-29jan2021.pdf. Accessed 24 March 2021.

Camargo, W. X. (2012). *Circulando entre práticas esportivas e sexuais: etnografia em competições mundiais esportivas LGBTs.* Doctoral dissertation, Universidade Federal de Santa Catarina, Florianópolis. https://repositorio.ufsc.br/xmlui/handle/123456789/96147

Camargo, W. X. (2017). *Ocupa Pacaembu: futebol de rua, arte, vivências. Ludopedio, São Paulo, 99*(3). https://www.ludopedio.com.br/arquibancada/ocupa-pacaembu/. Accessed 27 April 2020.

Camargo, W. X. (2020). Dimensões de gênero e os múltiplos futebóis no Brasil. In S. S. Giglio & M. W. Proni (orgs.), *O Futebol nas Ciências Humanas no Brasil* (pp. 589–604). Editora da Unicamp.

Connell, R. (1995). *Masculinities.* University of California.

Messner, M. (1989). Masculinities and athletic carreers. *Gender & Society, 3*(1), 71–88. https://www.jstor.org/stable/190040

Repolês, S. (2017). *Recalculando rotas: uma etnografia sobre trânsitos de corpos, afetos e sexualidades em vivências transmasculinas.* Master dissertation, Universidade Federal de Minas Gerais, Belo Horizonte.

Silvestrin, J. P., & Fernandez-Vaz, A. (2020). Meninos Bons de Bola: transmasculinidades em quadra. *CSOnline, 31,* 158–167. https://doi.org/10.34019/1981-2140.2020.30498

Symons, C. (2004). *The Gay Games: The play of sexuality, sport and community.* Doctoral dissertation, Victoria University, Melbourne, Victoria. https://vuir.vu.edu.au/15707/

Travers, A. (2006). Queering sport: Lesbian softball leagues and the transgender challenge. *International Review for the Sociology of Sport, 41*(4), 431–446. https://doi.org/10.1177/1012690207078070

CHAPTER 10

Educational Trajectories and Participation of Transgender Women in Sports in Argentina

Magalí Pérez-Riedel and Pablo Ariel Scharagrodsky

INTRODUCTION

Evidence suggests that both education and sports rely on the construction and the exclusion of those who do not fit the category of normalcy or sameness. The 'others,' those who do not fit the norm, are therefore symbolically and materially excluded normative values. Mocha Celis secondary school aims to end that exclusion.

Mocha Celis is the name of an Argentine secondary school for adults that is open and welcoming to the transgender community. Its goal is to help educate those that were marginalized by the normative school system and it is the first Latin American school of its kind.

M. Pérez-Riedel (✉) · P. A. Scharagrodsky
Universidad Nacional de La Plata, La Plata, Argentina

Universidad Nacional de Quilmes, Bernal, Argentina

P. A. Scharagrodsky
e-mail: pas@unq.edu.ar

J. Piedra and E. Anderson (eds.), *Lesbian, Gay, and Transgender Athletes in Latin America*, Palgrave Studies in Masculinity, Sport and Exercise, https://doi.org/10.1007/978-3-030-87375-2_10

By employing qualitative research methods, this chapter provides an overview of the educational trajectories and experiences of transgender women who were attending the Mocha Celis school. A total of ten semi-structured interviews were conducted between August and October 2016. Five transgender women who were attending the Mocha Celis school were interviewed in-depth. Additionally, the principal and four teachers were interviewed to gather information about their students, the school curricula, and their representations on the lives and educational trajectories of their transgender students.

The research questions are as follows: (1) What are the discursive representations about sports of the transgender students of the Mocha Celis secondary school?; (2) How would they describe their educational trajectories?; (3) What are their past experiences related to sports in school?; and (4) How do they feel about discriminatory songs, violent practices, and strict dress-codes when watching or listening to sports games in the media? The findings of this paper should make an important contribution to the field of inclusive education by shedding light on the limitations and challenges faced by transgender women in school and on the opportunities, possibilities, and practices of resistance that stem from this popular school.

The First Secondary School for Trans People in Latin America

Mocha Celis secondary school opened its doors in Buenos Aires (Argentina) in 2012. It is named after a *travesti*[1] who was an activist that was killed in 1996. This public school aims to include (but is not limited to) young transgenders that are 16 years old or more. It is broadly known that these people had been historically expelled and excluded from education: only 20% of *travesti* and transgender women were able to attend school, 80% of them are sex workers, and their average lifespan is 35 years (Berkins, 2006; Ministerio Público de la Defensa, 2017).

Researcher and politician, Diana Maffía, who was part of the launch of the school, said that 'it is a kind of highly inclusive education and it reaches sectors that are excluded from formal education. The idea of it being inclusive of all sexual identities is very important because, according to all the research we conducted, one of the first consequences of *travestismo* [being travesti] is school desertion' (Maffía, quoted by Lorea, 2011).

Indeed, the goal of the Mocha Celis school is to create a learning environment that allows students to improve their living conditions and job opportunities so as to overturn their conditions of prostitution, violence, and abandonment. It also seeks to encourage them to take part in worker-owned cooperatives. Hence, its curricula include subjects from areas such as social science, communication and language, as well as vocational courses. Being a school for adults, they do not have subjects such as sports or Physical Education. According to one of the teachers interviewed, the vast majority of their students are *travesti* women: they are the main victims of the cisheteronormative educational system and its exclusionary practices. Scharagrodsky (2020) argues that the public space and educational institutions are portrayed as hostile places. In most cases, 'the transgender and *travesti* populations experience situations of violence on public roads in general (88%) and in the neighborhood of residence in particular (63%). Other places were school (53%), police station (52%), home (45%), and work and public transport, both with 43%.'

Scharagrodsky (2020, p. 4) also finds that those trans women who 'assumed their gender identity at the age of 13 or earlier have a level of studies lower than a complete secondary school, by 69.6%. Something similar happens with those who assumed their gender identity between the ages of 14 and 18. Those who manifested their gender identity at the age of 19 or more have reached the complete secondary level or more by 74.2%' (Scharagrodsky, 2020, p. 4). In other words, those who hide their gender identity in Argentine schools have a greater chance of not being 'offside.'

Many of these women come from other Latin American countries and work on the streets. The teacher adds that this school, 'was not thought to exclude people but rather as a space that promotes diversity: a place free of discrimination, sexism, and stigmatization.' She adds: 'It has been said that it is a school for "*travesti* girls," but there are trans men, trans women, transsexuals – there are many different ways to name and to perceive oneself' (Teacher 1).

Most of the Mocha Celis's teachers are very committed to this school. Teacher, Augustin Fuchs, argues that in public schools, there is no questioning of topics such as gender and sports, doing Physical Education separately, or using gendered bathrooms. 'This is all taught from a heteronormative and binary point of view' (Fuchs, quoted in Dema, 2012). This is possibly the reason why one of the symbols of the school is an altered image of former Argentine president, Domingo Sarmiento.

This politician is portrayed with a blonde wig and make up. This subversive practice invites people to question some of the traditional and classical icons of the (white, phallic, bourgeois, and heteronormative) modern educational system while also shedding light on those identities that traditional educational institutions have silenced, excluded, and oppressed (Scharagrodsky, 2020).

Methods

This research took place during the second semester of 2016. We adopted a qualitative and interpretive approach (Vasilachis de Gialdino, 2007). On the one hand, we collected information and references through the search, gathering, organization, selection, and analysis of documentary and bibliographical material pertaining to the school. On the other hand, we conducted semi-structured interviews as a data collection technique to learn about the discursive representations and the educational trajectories of the trans students of the Mocha Celis secondary school. The aim of these interviews was also to learn about their past experiences of trans women regarding sports and about their educational trajectories.

The sampling that we selected was non-probabilistic, although we were selective when choosing our interviewees. As agreed with the principals, we chose to interview trans women students who were adults who were between 25 and 40 years old, and who were regular students of the second year. We chose to withhold their identity to protect their privacy. We also interviewed teachers with the highest levels of seniority in the institution, including two transgender teachers.

Challenging Compulsory Heterosexuality in Sports

One of the founders of the field of the sociology of sports, Eric Dunning, pointed out in one of his classic texts that the space of sports was built in England as a space reserved for men, used to claim the male hegemony and the superiority (Dunning, 1993; Elias & Dunning, 1996). There is no doubt that between the middle of the nineteenth century and most of the twentieth century sports in the Western World have contributed to the definition of a particular masculine identity (virile, active, successful, competitive, athletic, symmetrical, confident, vigorous, and with predominance in the public space); and by exclusion or segregation, a particular feminine identity (coy, passive, abnegated, graceful, elegant, and, fundamentally, held back in the private and domestic sphere) (Hau, 2003; Mosse, 2000; Park, 1987). This division was enhanced by a bourgeois colonial and imperial supremacy based on a specific type of gendered (and racialized) dominance, segregating those who were defined as 'deviant' by certain masculine phallocentric white, elite ideals because they did not follow the script of what was socially expected for women and men (Mangan & Mckenzie, 2008; Mosse, 2000; Park, 2007). In spite of some forms of resistance, this process was installed with strength during most of the twentieth century (Nye, 2007; Tumblety, 2013).

This binary and dual logic was a classic in the heterogeneous Argentine sports universe, not only thanks to the legitimation generated from the bio-medical episteme (anatomy, physiological, anthropometry, biometrics, endocrinology, etc.) (Reggiani, 2017; Scharagrodsky, 2018), but rather thanks to moral discourses sedimented on religious traditions, Hispanic heritages, and alliances between certain social sectors from several coups d'état or military dictatorships (Barrancos et al., 2014). This consolidated the circulation of a logic of possible desires that were appropriate and thinkable: heterosexuality was the only alternative of desire that was possible and desirable. This gained strength in the world of sports while excluding, silencing, and forgetting those other ways of feeling, of being, and of occupying the social world.

This matrix of thought about the bodies, the genders, the sexualities, the pleasures, and the desires excluded a diverse group of identities such as, for example, trans people. As a student of the Mocha Celis says: 'sports were never keen on trans identities' (Student 1). Indeed, the problem has never been sports themselves as they are social practices like any other. But the issue here are the logics of sense and meaning that they transmitted (and transmitting) about sexual difference, or about how it should be interpreted and about which bodies are privileged when it comes down to having access to and enjoying certain practices and which bodies are labeled as abject. 'Sports can build stereotype-free spaces, but not many [people] care about that,' Student 2 claims.

Suffering, pain, discomfort, suffering, dissatisfaction, discrimination, or ridicule are some of the words used by trans students to refer to their sports experiences outside and, especially, within the modern educational institutions. Most of the reflections are condensed in the following statement: 'Sports for me were always very exclusionary' (Student 1). Trans interviewees agreed that they were obliged to practice sports in schools:

'I was forced to do things that I did not like, for example, playing ball at school' (Student 3). If she refused, she would get physically punished, she said.

This way, sports and heteronormativity become the hegemonic discursive/epistemic model that assumes that for sport bodies to be consistent in their appearance, in their rules of etiquette and dress, in their aesthetics, in their gestures, and in their physical silhouette, they must have a stable sex expressed through a stable gender that is defined historically and by opposition through compulsory heterosexual practice. In doing so, it excludes other possible alternatives of thinking, experiencing, and inhabiting the bodies in motion.

One of the occupational groups that is mentioned by all the interviewees who went through the process of schooling are Physical Education teachers. It is said that they were 'super sexist and discriminating' (Student 3), as well as punitive, as, 'they forced me to play' (Student 4).

'They wanted to make me play football and I did not want to,' 'football players are very sexist but behind closed doors they are no longer sexist,' 'in school, I did not want to play football with boys and they forced me' (Students 1, 4, and 5); 'I played football with friends and it amused me, but at school I suffered,' 'they disqualify the fag with a football.' Another said, 'I was forced to do things I did not like, for example, to play ball. That is the worst memory I have of school,' 'after I got hit with a ball in the face, I did not play football anymore' (Students 2 and 3). In short, PE teachers 'are not prepared for or accepting of trans students' (Student 5). This characterization of this group of teachers goes hand in hand with the representation of the Principal of the secondary school Mocha Celis, Francisco Quiñones. He argues that PE is the educational discipline that has caused the most discrimination and pain among trans people.

EMOTIONS, SPORTS, SCHOOL, AND TRANS WOMEN

When remembering and evoking sports experiences at school, transgender women's memories were linked to the expression of certain emotions. Among them, fear and discomfort stood out. One of the emotional policies that has operated in the sports experiences of the interviewees has been that of *fear*. It has been used to group and differentiate 'us' from 'others.' This emotional politics, which is intentional, objectifying, and violently fabricated, appears in most of the interviews. One of the interviewees says: 'At school, there was a football field. Every week, we went there for an hour. Going there made me terribly anxious. When I approached the field, the anxiety turned into fear and many times I was paralyzed.' She adds: 'To "get away" and not be a threat, the best thing was to remain seated (...) on the edge of the field and go as unnoticed as possible while my teammates played, shouted, and had fun' (Student 2).

Here, paralysis, rejection, and fear operated and were associated with a certain space (the football field) and with certain sports practices. But fear is not an inherent characteristic of bodies, spaces, or practices, but it inhabits the movement of some bodies in public space (Ahmed, 2015). The regulation of bodies in space through the unequal distribution of fear allows spaces to become territories, claimed as rights by some bodies and not others (Ahmed, 2015, p. 118).

This unequal distribution of fear is a complex and violent cultural process that is socially and politically produced. It is embedded and solidified in the body of sexual dissidents and it is one of the many coercive effects of patriarchal and heteronormative norms that operate to create a distinction between those who are 'threatened' and those who are a threat (Ahmed, 2015). A trans student says: 'In school, I was scared of some places. I learned that I could not move freely because I ran the risk of being the victim of jokes, insults or even physical threats, such as in bathrooms and obviously the places where we practiced sports' (Student 1).

In these interviews, fear is constructed and gains meaning through social imaginary and interaction. Emotions such as fear are not in the spaces or in the practices. Fear appears in the interaction between two or more people. These emotional teachings and learnings, which continue to be strongly installed and naturalized in contemporary societies, have caused a great deal of pain and hostility toward most of our interviewees at school and sports.

Along with the production of fear, most of the interviewees talked of feeling uncomfortable when practicing certain sports or kinetic experiences in schools: 'I remember that Jorge, the gymnastics teacher, did not say anything when the kids laughed at how I moved or how I kicked the ball. I suffered a lot. There were uncomfortable and violent situations' (Student 2). Other researchers who studied the relation between the trans community and Physical Education confirm the existence of this feeling of fear and discomfort (Martínez & Vidal-Ortiz, 2018). These feelings escaped the spheres of sports and Physical Education and are still embedded in the entire Argentine school system. According to Scharagrodsky (2020), recent statistics on the situation of transgender women in Buenos Aires indicate that despite the desire of a good part of the trans community to continue studying, the educational institution continues to be represented as an inhospitable and hostile space.

CONTRADICTIONS AND AMBIVALENCES ABOUT THE CORPOREAL MODELS BUILT BY SPORTS

The experience with the sports universe and, especially, with Physical Education in modern educational institutions is not characterized as pleasurable or gratifying because it is saturated with a suffocating, stereotyping, hierarchical, and excluding heteronormative regime (Scharagrodsky, 2019). However, one interesting finding is that our interviewees affirm that they currently practice sports and Physical Education.

Here, sports acquire different meanings, attributes, and functions. On the one hand, there are those trans women who associate sports with health, in contrast with the times in which the bodies were modified with risky procedures like, for example, the use of injections of oil or silicone to beautify certain parts of the body, or injections of hormones from illegal markets, without prior medical advice. According to one of the female transgender teachers, 'Before it was "in" to inject yourself. Now, not so much. The idea is to do something healthy: sports and food' (Teacher 2). On the other hand, three interviewees claim to specialize in sports, such as personal defense, boxing, and kickboxing.

In the first case, body care and health refers to aerobic gymnastics, swimming, or cycling, to look after certain parts of the body, like 'flattening the abdomen,' 'to have a bigger bum,' 'to tone up,' 'to have certain parts of the body "toned up" but not too much [because] having big arms is not too favorable' (Students 1 and 5). This regionalization of the body is constituted from a certain physical hierarchy. An arbitrary body topography is constituted as true and desirable, as an ideal type of body.

In this case, through physical exercise or sports practice, trans girls value the aesthetics, presentation, certain rules of etiquette and beauty that are deemed traditionally 'feminine.' In this way, the trans body is constructed and modeled according to certain criteria and, in many cases, they do not question the reifying dictatorship of the heteronormative beauty constructed by and from a hierarchical logic. Although trans bodies are diverse and challenge the imagery of the traditional sex-gender system, redefining the possibilities of the body and of certain body parts and installing new senses of pleasure and enjoyment; the fictional projection of certain body models as aesthetic ideals, in many cases, when incarnated, generates more reification than resistances to the dominant body model.

In the second case, sports choices and consumption are linked to a varied universe of practices among which some stand out: karate, boxing, and self-defense. Trans women practice these sports 'to feel more safe,' 'to know how to defend myself,' and 'to be alert' (Students 2 and 4). Consequently, these practices have a clear instrumental character with a specific purpose: to defend themselves against the frequent verbal and physical aggressions of the wider society. The meanings and the choice of these sports are not linked to the pleasure or the enjoyment or to spend a good time, but they have a clear mediating and instrumental function. In these cases, sports become a means and not an end in themselves.

This function is supported by one of the students who is a kickboxing teacher.

In any case, professional football is the sport that is consumed and televised the most in Argentina. It is clearly saturated with a homophobic logic (Scharagrodsky, 2003). Most of the football songs denigrate the other through the term *puto* ('fag'). In the particular case of the word *puto*, not only it is used to humiliate and offend a person or a rival team, but also as a way to reaffirm the (heterosexual) masculinity that depends on depriving the others from its own (Scharagrodsky, 2003).

MOCHA CELIS SCHOOL AS A PLACE
OF RESISTANCE AND AMBIGUITIES

Mocha Celis school is the first openly inclusive public institution in Argentina to guarantee the human rights and educational, cultural, social, and political rights of *travesti*, transgender, transsexual people, homosexuals, and other groups that have historically been deliberately excluded and doomed to school failure in the complex modern educational universe. Not only does it set itself apart from the rest of the schools. In doing so, its political-educational proposal denounces the hierarchical, classifying, and exclusionary oppositional binaries of modern educational institutions in Argentina.

With nuances, and not without internal tensions, the Mocha Celis assumes a clear political position by striving for empowerment and the 'real' materialization of equal social, cultural, political, legal, and economic opportunities: not only does the school help trans students learn and get a school diploma but it also gives them the vocational knowledge they need to secure formal jobs. Also, it challenges the idea of the body as something merely organic, fixed, universal, and ahistorical. It regards it as a field of dispute in which different social actors and discourses try to impose certain meanings that are often coercive on the sexual materiality. It also de-naturalizes the notions of gender and sexuality as something fixed and already stable. It questions the biological determinism that involves relations and mechanical and linear processes according to the sexed body that one 'has got.' It rejects and disregards the subordination of sub-alternated sexual groups as something natural. It identifies the features of the patriarchal oppression that lessen and stigmatize trans groups. And it opposes certain imageries that link trans groups with deviance, perversion, excess, immorality, and abnormality by questioning the dominant phallocentric sexual morality.

In regard to the heterogeneous universe of sports, most of the interviewees question the exclusionary and stigmatizing meanings of the practices of sports that they have consumed or experimented throughout their educational trajectories. Pain, discomfort, and fear were some of the many emotions that trans women have always associated with sports. Nonetheless, most of them wish they could give a new meaning to these representations and get their bodies in shape, whether it is doing Physical Education or sports. Some of them accomplish so.

The contradictions and ambivalences about the models of bodies that are built from sports continue to circulate as most of the purposes that were expressed by the trans students: they reproduce the hegemonic corporeal model that reifies the female bodies by requesting them to adapt to a fixed criterion of aesthetics and beauty that oppresses them more than what it frees them. These contradictions can also be found in the judicial level: although transgender women are legally entitled to participate 'freely' in sports, at the same time, the difficulties, the tensions, and the stigmatizations are still present in the 'real life.'

In sum, the aim of this paper was to study the representations of past sport practices and the educational trajectories of the transgender women who attend the Mocha Celis school. The school faces the challenge of trying to erode the exclusionary aspects of sports, but it should do so by including sports and PE into their curriculum. In order to foster the rights to education, sexual justice, and dignity of their transgender students and the trans community as a whole, its curricular policy needs to have a stronger emphasis on sports issues not only as a historically situated social practice but rather as a field of dispute where different social actors try to impose certain meanings about the body, sexuality, emotion, pleasure, and desire.

Physical Education and sports should be mandatory in the curriculum of secondary schools for adults, such as the Mocha Celis. While the school manages to disrupt many of the gender and sexual orders, when it comes down to sports and PE there is still a lot of learning and training left to do.

In spite of all the forms of resistance, the trans population is losing in the field of sports by far. This loss is not only corporeal but it is essentially political and ethical. The hope of building sport practices that are more just, democratic, inclusive, empathetic, and respectful of the differences has a name in Argentine education: it is Mocha Celis.

Note

1. In Argentina, a 'travesti' is a transgender or transsexual woman. It's a term used to refer both to a gender identity and a gender expression but it is also a form of political resistance (Di Pietro, 2015). The term is sometimes used as an insult, but on other occasions it is positively re-appropriated by trans women as a means of political-identity reaffirmation.

References

Ahmed, S. (2015). *La política cultural de las emociones*. Universidad Nacional Autónoma de México.

Barrancos, D., Guy, D., & Valobra, A. (Eds.). (2014). *Moralidades y comportamientos sexuales. Argentina (1880–2011)*. Biblos.

Berkins, L. (2006). *La gesta del nombre propio*. Madres de Plaza de Mayo.

Dema, V. (2012, February 29). Nace el primer bachillerato para travestis. *Boquitas pintadas*. https://origenblogs.lanacion.com.ar/boquitas-pintadas/agenda/nace-el-primer-bachillerato-para-travestis. Accessed 10 December 2020.

Di Pietro, P. (2015). Andar de costado: Racialización, sexualidad y la descolonización del mundo travesti en Buenos Aires. In R. M. Ferrera-Balanquet (Ed.), *Andar Erótico Decolonial* (pp. 131–152). Ediciones del Signo.

Dunning, E. (1993). *Reflexiones sociológicas sobre el deporte, la violencia y la civilización. Materiales de Sociología del Deporte*. La Piqueta.

Elias, E., & Dunning, E. (1996). El deporte como coto masculino: Notas sobre las fuentes sociales de la identidad masculina y sus transformaciones. In N. Elias & E. Dunning (Eds.), *Deporte y ocio en el proceso de la civilización* (pp. 323–342). FCE.

Hau, M. (2003). *The cult of health and beauty in Germany: A social history, 1890–1930*. University of Chicago Press.

Lorea, J. (2011, December 26). El saber travestido. *El gran otro*. http://elgranotro.com.ar/el-saber-travestido. Accessed 10 December 2020.

Mangan, J. A., & McKenzie, C. (2008). 'Duty unto death', the sacrificial warrior: English middle class masculinity and militarism in the age of new imperialism. *International Journal of the History of Sport, 25*(9), 1080–1105. https://doi.org/10.1080/09523360802166105

Martínez, J. & Vidal-Ortiz, S. (Eds.). (2018). *Travar el saber: Educación de personas trans y travestis en Argentina*. Edulp.

Ministerio Público de la Defensa. (2017). *La Revolución de las Mariposas: a diez años de La gesta del nombre propio*.

Mosse, G. (2000). *La imagen del hombre. La creación de la masculinidad moderna*. Talasa.

Nye, R. A. (2007). Western masculinities in war and peace. *American Historical Review, 112*(2), 417–438.

Park, R. J. (1987). Physiologists, physicians and physical educators: Nineteenth century Biology and exercise, hygienic and educative. *Journal of Sport History, 14*(1), 28–60. https://doi.org/10.1080/09523360701619030

Park, R. J. (2007). Biological thought, athletics and the formation of a 'man of character': 1830–1900. *International Journal of the History of Sport, 24*(12), 1543–1569. https://doi.org/10.1080/09523360701618982

Reggiani, A. H. (2017). Four fitness and the national body: Modernity, physical culture and gender, 1930–1945. In B. Bryce & D. M. K. Sheinin (Eds.), *Making citizens in Argentina* (pp. 83–101). University of Pittsburgh Press. https://doi.org/10.2307/j.ctt1r69xtk.8

Scharagrodsky, P. (2003). Los graffitis y los cantitos futboleros platenses (o acerca del proceso de configuración de diversas masculinidades). *Oficios Terrestres, 13*(1), 161–174.

Scharagrodsky, P. (2018). El padre de la medicina deportiva argentina o acerca de cómo fabricar campeones, décadas del '20 y '30, siglo XX [The father of Argentine sports medicine or about how to 'manufacture' champions (1920s and 1930s)]. *Recorde: Revista de História do Esporte, 11*(2), 1–29.

Scharagrodsky, P. (2019). Trans-formando el espacio educativo y deportivo. El caso de la comunidad trans en la capital argentina. *Revista Investiga+, 2*(2), 15–35.

Scharagrodsky, P. (2020). *(Trans)formando los géneros y las sexualidades en las instituciones educativas.* Papeles de coyuntura. IdHICS, UNLP. http://idihcs.fahce.unlp.edu.ar/pephpp/trans-formando-los-generos-y-las-sexualidades-en-las-instituciones-educativas/

Tumblety, J. (2013). *Remaking the male body: Masculinity and the uses of physical culture in interwar and vichy France.* Oxford University Press.

Vasilachis de Gialdino, I. (2007). *Estrategias de investigación cualitativa.* Gedisa.

INDEX

J. Piedra and E. Anderson (eds.), *Lesbian, Gay, and Transgender Athletes in Latin America*, Palgrave Studies in Masculinity, Sport and Exercise, https://doi.org/10.1007/978-3-030-87375-2

Printed by Printforce, United Kingdom